PRAISE FOR *PURSUING WISDOM*

"There is no telling how many problems and how much suffering could have been avoided if people had exercised wisdom. This primer provides a clarion call and hope for wisdom's return to the public square. Wisdom is now made simple and accessible to leaders and learners thanks to this scholarly informed treatise on the nature of wisdom."

—**Barbara Cockerham**, retired professor, K–12
teacher and administrator, mentor

"Wisdom is the essential ingredient to greatness most lacking in the world today in every sphere of influence. The authors not only accomplish their objective set forth in the preface to help anyone to become astute lovers and doers of wisdom but also provide a model for the common ground where the great issues of our day can be resolved."

—**Honorable Will Dodson**, senior retired judge, Ninth
Administrative Judicial Region of Texas

"This book is life changing. It is a well-written, professorial presentation about wisdom and how to attain it. It is one of those 'must-read' books for anyone who wants to take wisdom seriously and become especially skilled at leading and developing leaders, from parents to presidents."

—**Paul Kienel**, founder, Association of Christian Schools International

"This marvelously written volume, exploring various conceptions of wisdom, is aptly called a primer in both dictionary definitions of this term. It succeeds in being both an accessible elementary book for teaching and a book covering the core principles needed for a robust understanding and application of wisdom in personal and civic life. The authors examine the nature and role of wisdom in three fields: in philosophy where wisdom is an intellectual and moral virtue, in theology where wisdom results from encounters with transcendental reality interpreted by sacred texts, and in empirical inquiry where wisdom is the practical understanding and successful navigation of competing ethical values and priorities. The world would be a better place if leaders in business, politics, religion, and education attended closely to this work."

—**Douglas E. Mitchell**, professor, Graduate Division,
University of California, Riverside

"I am excited about this opportunity to further explore wisdom from the lenses of a 40-year public safety leader, husband, father, coach and mentor. I'm excited to have a one-stop book of philosophy, theology, and empirical tradition that I can dive into and take small bites to learn wisdom for life. As I press through my final chapter as a public service leader (fire chief), this book will give me and others the tools to summarize the so-often mystical components of wisdom that are required to truly be successful in life."
—**Michael D. Moore**, MPA, EFO; fire chief, Riverside City Fire Department

"*Pursuing Wisdom* is unique, insightful, and takes a new perspective on wisdom and the practical application to leadership. This is a must-read primer that breaks down the BIG idea of what wisdom is into everyday bits, so all of us can live and lead wisely."
—**Jenny Nuccio**, founder and CEO of Imani Collective

"Wisdom, the first virtue on which all others hinge, is the *sine qua non* of exemplary leadership and necessary for society to function properly and thrive. This primer provides a clear and cogent model of wisdom with illuminating examples for readers to become the sophisticated and virtuous leaders that society desperately longs for and needs. The primer provides a word to the wise and should be assigned reading for all emerging and established leaders."
—**Jay Orr**, dean, Community & Global Claremont Graduate University; former county executive officer, Riverside County

"In *Pursuing Wisdom: A Primer for Leaders and Learners*, the authors expose the reader to a robust consideration of wisdom and its relationship to Truth and truth. The authors masterfully interweave theory and practice by exploring common ground and comparing divergent execution among a variety of philosophical, theological, and empirical perspectives. Using a collection of real-life narratives and crafted scenarios, the book helps readers better understand that 'knowing truth and practicing wisdom involve different combinations of humility, confidence, faith, and reason regarding truth claims and corresponding judgments.' This is an intelligently accessible book that skillfully balances the why and how of pursuing wisdom."
—**Andrea Scott**, provost, George Fox University

"The authors do an incredible job of providing a holistic approach, one that demonstrates how all philosophical, theological, and empirical traditions share striking similarities in their understandings of the nature of wisdom. Humanity's on-going search for truth through the ages, as related by the authors, should guide and inspire us all."

—**Donald C. Simmons, Jr.**, director of pastoral care and chair, medical ethics, North Mississippi Health System; former dean, chair, and professor of leadership and public service, McGovern Center for Leadership and Public Service, Dakota Wesleyan University

"The book is a godsend for educators. It provides new, yet timeless, insights on the nature of wisdom and how to elevate the wisdom quotients in schools and society and make the world a better place."

—**Heather William**, executive director, Personnel Services, Riverside County Office of Education

"Wisdom appears to be in short supply among today's leaders. This excellent book examines wisdom through multiple perspectives arriving at a model to understand, acquire, practice, and teach wisdom. I highly recommend it to leaders and learners as a helpful tool to bring more wisdom to our world."

—**John Jacob Zucker Gardiner**, emeritus professor of leadership, Seattle University

PURSUING
WISDOM

PURSUING WISDOM
A PRIMER FOR LEADERS AND LEARNERS

John R. Shoup, Troy W. Hinrichs,
and Jacqueline N. Gustafson
Dr. Paul & Annie Kienel Leadership Institute

ROWMAN & LITTLEFIELD
Lanham • Boulder • New York • London

Acquisitions Editor: Natalie Mandziuk
Acquisitions Assistant: Sylvia Landis
Sales and Marketing Inquiries: textbooks@rowman.com

Credits and acknowledgments for material borrowed from other sources, and reproduced with permission, appear on the appropriate pages within the text.

Published by Rowman & Littlefield
An imprint of The Rowman & Littlefield Publishing Group, Inc.
4501 Forbes Boulevard, Suite 200, Lanham, Maryland 20706
www.rowman.com

86-90 Paul Street, London EC2A 4NE, United Kingdom

Copyright © 2022 by The Rowman & Littlefield Publishing Group, Inc.

British Library Cataloguing in Publication Information Available

Library of Congress Cataloging-in-Publication Data Is Available

ISBN: 978-1-5381-5984-2 (cloth : alk. paper)
ISBN: 978-1-5381-5985-9 (pbk. : alk. paper)
ISBN: 978-1-5381-5986-6 (electronic)

∞™ The paper used in this publication meets the minimum requirements of American National Standard for Information Sciences—Permanence of Paper for Printed Library Materials, ANSI/NISO Z39.48-1992.

CONTENTS

PREFACE

Wisdom, the highest level of enlightenment, is noticeably rare among leaders and professionals serving in business, education, government, health, law, media, ministry, sports, and society at large. Wisdom is critical if leaders and followers are to lead and follow well. Stories of leaders' lack of discernment and sound judgment abound throughout history and all too often in current events. Comments such as "What were they thinking?" and "Why did they do that?" reveal that wisdom is often painfully lacking when it comes to making decisions and exercising leadership. While wisdom "shouts out in the street" and "lifts her voice in the square," even to the naïve and foolish (Proverbs 1:20–22), it seems that only a few people take up the invitation to acquire and practice it.

Part of the challenge is that the mystique often associated with wisdom gives the impression that it is reserved for the few or too great of an endeavor or status for mere mortals. Wisdom also competes with enticing false comforts associated with pleasure, possessions, and prestige, making it the path less traveled. Schools do not generally promote wisdom given their emphasis on transferring knowledge and conforming students to scripted answers and norms. Organizations with their singular missions and conditioned overreliance on policies and procedures make wisdom seem unnecessary, if not unwelcomed, in the workplace. Governments replace the need for individual wisdom when they over-legislate and regulate behaviors. Norms, rules, policies, procedures, and laws are necessary, but when they are too rigid and excessive, they become contributing factors to the general absence of wisdom in society.

A primary reason that wisdom is not as common as it could and should be is because most people do not understand what wisdom is and consequently how to acquire, practice, and teach it. Philosophers, theologians, and social scientists have not made the topic easily accessible for others to understand. Philosophers, the so-called experts on wisdom, are often too lengthy and abstract in their teachings on wisdom. Theologians, the so-called masters of wisdom, make it sound like it is only for the religiously motivated and enlightened. Social scientists, so-called students of wisdom, tend to be overly technical and almost formulaic in their attempts to quantify and qualify wisdom. Each tradition provides valuable insights on the nature of wisdom, but are usually framed only for fellow acolytes, making wisdom often unappealing and inaccessible to the uninitiated. In other words, people are good at talking to others in their professional circles, but they fail to communicate with others outside those circles.

What is amazing is that each tradition teaches similar things about the nature of wisdom, something often missed for reasons just cited. Unsurprisingly, an accurate, clear, and useful model of wisdom emerges when the teaching and research on wisdom from the philosophical, theological, and empirical traditions are integrated. This primer explores the nature of wisdom from the philosophical, theological, and empirical perspectives and synthesizes the learning into a simple and cohesive model for students, parents, educators, professionals, leaders, and everyone else to use in order to live and lead wisely.

Chapter 1 begins with an overview of the field of philosophy and its love affair with wisdom. The chapter walks the readers through Boethius's *Consolation of Philosophy*, Plato's *Republic* and *The Laws*, Aristotle's *Nicomachean Ethics*, and Confucius's *Analects*. The chapter also references the works of Al-Farabi, the works of Avicenna, and Averroes's treatment of wisdom from the Golden Age of Islam. The chapter concludes with what these major philosophers had in common in their approaches to explain the nature of wisdom.

Chapter 2 begins with an introduction to theology. The chapter walks the readers through wisdom as described in the respective sacred texts of four major religions, the Vedas for Hinduism, the Hebrew Bible for Judaism, the Old and New Testaments for Christianity, and the Quran for Islam. The chapter concludes with how the different theological texts share similar approaches to the nature of wisdom, albeit with different content. Chapter 3 begins with an overview of the empirical tradition. The chapter describes the different research models on wisdom found in the social sciences: Ardelt's Three Dimensions of Wisdom, Baltes's Expert Theory, Sternberg's Balance Theory, and Peterson and Seligman's Character Strengths and Virtues. The chapter also reviews the hidden architecture governing all complex adaptive systems as described in complexity theory and makes corresponding connections to and among the models previously identified to reveal similar understandings on the nature of practical wisdom.

Chapter 4 synthesizes the findings from the previous chapters to reveal how the philosophical, theological, and empirical traditions share striking similarities in their understandings of the nature of wisdom. The chapter provides a cohesive model of wisdom and several examples that highlight the nature of wisdom as defined in the chapter. The primer concludes with corresponding principles on how to acquire, practice, and teach wisdom.

Professional philosophers, theologians, and social scientists may find a primer on wisdom problematic, if not impossible. Admittedly, a primer on wisdom runs the risk of oversimplifying a rich tradition. This concern is mitigated as this primer is on the nature of wisdom—its purpose, structure, and elements, not the content of wisdom—specific worldview assumptions, truth claims, goals, and ranking of values. What also makes this primer a valid endeavor is that it provides a synthesis of wisdom from representative and seminal philosophical and theological texts and empirical studies, eliminating the requirement to read every major work in the corpus. A third mitigation is this primer does not claim to be a full treatise on wisdom, but rather an introductory read that encourages additional love for and study of wisdom. More importantly, this primer is designed to equip emerging and established leaders across all professions and disciplines with a foundational understanding of wisdom necessary for them to acquire, practice, and teach wisdom.

This primer is also unique in that it walks the reader through a representative sample of classical philosophical and sacred texts and empirical studies in lieu of summaries of major sources of wisdom. As a result, the primer orients the readers to think like philosophers, theologians, and social scientists by shepherding them through the logic and content of the cited texts and research. What also sets this primer apart is its brevity without compromise to substance. This primer demonstrates that the complex can be made relatively simple, brevity does not preclude profundity, and profundity at times requires brevity. The content, format, and size of this primer makes it an inviting and informative read for leaders who want to understand, acquire, practice, and teach wisdom.

The value and nature of wisdom is captured in a dialogue between the philosopher Socrates and his friend Phaedrus. Socrates was pondering on a moniker for truth seekers and defenders, those who are "to be called, not only poets, orators, and legislators, but are worthy of a higher name that is befitting the serious pursuit of their life." Phaedrus asked Socrates what name he would assign to such people, and Socrates replied, "Wise, I may not call them; for that is a great name which belongs to God alone,—lovers of wisdom or philosophers is their modest and befitting title."[1]

May this primer serve you well to become astute lovers and doers of wisdom.

ACKNOWLEDGMENTS

Special acknowledgment and thank-you to:

- The benefactors of the Dr. Paul & Annie Kienel Leadership Institute, who made it possible for the Institute Fellows to think, write, and teach on wisdom.
- Abigail Bello and Sara Guardado, for their invaluable assistance with the manuscript.
- Natalie Mandziuk, for her supportive guidance in bringing this book to its final form.

1

PHILOSOPHICAL PERSPECTIVES ON WISDOM

Philosophy literally means the love (*philos*) of wisdom (*sophia*). As lovers of wisdom, philosophers address the fundamental questions of life related to meaning and purpose, the nature of knowing, and the essence of beauty and goodness. The skilled philosophers use logic to infer cohesive, comprehensive, congruent, and cogent answers that are rationally defensible regarding the nature and essence of truth, knowing truth, and human flourishing. As a result, philosophy is both a constructive (answering questions) and critical (questioning answers) endeavor that explores right thinking, feeling, and behaviors to live the "good" life.

Bertrand Russell, a prominent twentieth-century British philosopher and father of modern analytical philosophy, explained well the value of philosophy, distinguishing between the practical and philosophical mind. He candidly noted that "the man who has no tincture for philosophy goes through life imprisoned in the prejudices derived from common sense, from the habitual beliefs of his age or his nation, and from convictions which have grown up in his mind without the co-operation or consent of his deliberate reason."[1]

For Russell, philosophical contemplation enlightened the self and provided a renewing sense of wonder that was healthy for the soul. Russell summed up his discussion on the problems and value of philosophy, highlighting the merit of philosophical inquiry, "but above all because, through the greatness of the universe which philosophy contemplates, the mind is also rendered great, and becomes capable of that union with the universe which constitutes its highest good."[2]

There is a variety of approaches to the study of philosophy: geographical (Eastern and Western); methodological (analytical and continental); and taxonomical (metaphysics, epistemology, axiology, and logic). While Eastern philosophy tends to take a more holistic orientation, it has more similarities to Western thinking than differences. While analytical philosophy tends to focus on the logic of thinking and continental philosophy tends to focus on the narratives and content of thoughts, they are complementary in that one cannot exist without the other. The branches of philosophy, while interrelated, offer four useful and distinct categories:

- Metaphysics: What is the nature of reality?
- Epistemology: What is the nature of knowing?
- Axiology: What is the good?
  - Ethics: What is right behavior?
  - Aesthetics: What is beauty?
- Logic: What makes reasoning valid?

Rather than provide a comprehensive explanation of wisdom from a plethora of philosophers throughout the ages, a sample of writings was selected with priority consideration to seminal and/or most cited philosophers on the subject. As stated in the preface and throughout this primer, the learning focuses on the nature of wisdom and not the content of wisdom, hence it allows a few of the respected works to speak for the whole corpus. This chapter begins with one of the more famous, yet lesser-known to the general public, philosophers when it comes to the topic of wisdom—Boethius.

BOETHIUS

Medieval statesman, scholar, and philosopher Boethius (ca. 475–526 B.C.E.) provides an insightful starting point to frame the nature and promise of wisdom in the philosophical tradition. Boethius is often lost in the shadow of Socrates, Plato, and Aristotle, even though his works were equally as far-reaching. C. S. Lewis listed Boethius's *The Consolation of Philosophy* as one of the ten most influential books he had read.[3] Medieval literature scholar Edmund Reiss stated in his book, *Boethius*, that:

> Throughout the Middle Ages Boethius' *The Consolation of Philosophy* was quoted verbatim thousands of times in almost every context and paraphrased scores of thousands of times. . . . Boethius deserves to be remembered and indeed to be better known than he is, not only because he is one of the most important philosophers of the Western world but also because he is one of its most accomplished men of letters and poets.[4]

According to Russell: "[Boethius] would have been remarkable in any age, in the age which he lived, he is utterly amazing."[5]

Boethius enjoyed the fortunes of a privileged upbringing, a loving wife and children, and an enviable career in high public office as a scholar. He unexpectedly lost favor with his king, Theodoric the Great, as a victim of political intrigue and was unjustly imprisoned after being accused of treason under specious evidence. Boethius became depressed at his abrupt change in fortune, especially distressed that his exile was due to a baseless accusation. Seeking existential relief, Boethius returned to philosophy for consolation as a condemned prisoner. In this circumstance of unjust imprisonment, isolation, and ultimately his death, he wrote *The Consolation of Philosophy*.

The title of Boethius's *prosimetrum* (a combination of prose and poetry) revealed that philosophy is a solace for both the contented and the troubled souls in that it provides perspectives to rightly understand life. Boethius personified wisdom as a Lady who visits him in prison and comforts him in his hour of distress. He wrote:

> "But," she said, "it is time for medicine rather than complaint." Fixing me with her eyes, she said: "Are you not he who once was nourished by my milk and brought up on my food; who emerged from weakness to the strength of a virile soul? I gave you weapons that would have protected you with invincible power, if you had not thrown them away. Don't you recognize me? Why don't you speak? Is it shame or astonishment that makes you silent? . . ." When she saw that I was not only silent but struck dumb she gently laid her hand on my breast and said, "There is no danger. You are suffering merely from lethargy; the common illness of deceived minds. You have forgotten yourself a little,

but you will quickly be yourself when you recognize me. To bring you to your senses, I shall quickly wipe the dark cloud of mortal things from your eyes."[6]

The Consolation of Philosophy is an imaginary dialogue between Boethius and Lady Philosophy on how to make sense of life, especially when it goes unexpectedly wrong. Its style and content evoke aspects of Job, Ecclesiastes, Seneca, and Aristotle.[7] Lady Philosophy recalled for Boethius his upbringing in wisdom from the Stoics and other great teachers and chided him for becoming seduced and deceived by his previous good fortune to think meaning was found in personal blessings and professional successes. Lady Philosophy reminded Boethius that his plight in prison was not unique, as she recalled that wisdom has always been underappreciated and harassed, as evidenced by Socrates's death by hemlock and the torture of Zeno.[8] Boethius showed what history has proven, that wicked people make "impious attacks upon virtue" and "prevail against innocence."[9]

Boethius pondered where and how hope and meaning are found in injustice and asked "the cherisher of all virtues to tell him the truth."[10] The phrasing of the request reveals that wisdom cherishes the virtues and is the means to ultimate truth and, as noted later in the dialogue, it is the remedy for ignorance and imprisonment of the mind. The conversation continued with Lady Philosophy reviewing the false comforts associated with pleasure, fame, and wealth and how people are deceived to think that such pursuits can provide lasting happiness or ultimate meaning. She told Boethius not to value the baser things in life, but to turn toward reason (philosophy) and the heavens (theology), which govern the universe, to discern what the mind should ultimately dwell on and the volition should act upon. For Boethius, the answer was virtue, noting that "what is health to the soul but virtue? And what is sickness, but vice?"[11] Lady Philosophy reminded Boethius to "keep the middle path of strength and virtue, lest you be overwhelmed by misfortune or corrupted by pleasant fortune" as "all fortune which seems difficult, either exercises virtue, or corrects or punishes vice."[12]

The conversation explored next how and why evil exists, why bad things happen, and the nature and role of chance in human affairs. The dialogue highlighted the need for individuals to understand the mysteries of life and discern how to live wisely in harmony with natural and divine truths. Lady Philosophy reminded Boethius that Providence is not random, capricious fate, but that events are part of a comprehensive and beautiful plan not always evident from a temporal vantage point. That fate appears fickle belies the sense and expectation that life is coordinated at some level.

The final and all-encompassing lesson from Boethius was that "the better a man uses his reason, the freer he is: the more a man patterns his soul on divine thought, the freer he is. To will what the body desires is the highest degree of slavery; to will what God wills and to love what He loves is the highest form of liberty, and therefore happiness."[13] The *Consolation* made clear that wisdom is the pursuit of the highest good that invokes God's guidance. Lady Philosophy concluded, "Turn therefore from vice: ensue virtue: raise your soul to upright hopes: send up on high your prayers from earth. If you would be honest, great is the necessity enjoined upon your goodness since all you do is done before the eyes of an all-seeing Judge."[14]

For Boethius, wisdom requires the honest pursuit of the more transcendent perspectives. The best thoughts and actions out of the many that are available are those deemed worthier by an all-knowing Benevolent Judge. A contemporary message would be to live a life that would make family members proud.

It is worth noting that Boethius took time to describe in detail Lady Philosophy's appearance, attire, demeanor, and composure. The careful description conveyed that the fruit of wisdom is pure, peaceful, confident, endearing, and enduring. Wisdom's appearance alone made her venerable. The tenor of the dialogue also revealed that wisdom is a calm teacher who prompts inquiring minds to the more important questions, elucidating nuanced insights on the true and the good.

SOCRATES, PLATO, AND ARISTOTLE

Boethius did not define or describe what constituted virtue and vice. These concepts were already well-established ideas thanks to the work of centuries of philosophers familiar to Boethius's audiences, most notably Socrates, Plato, and Aristotle. Socrates, Plato, and Aristotle are grouped for this primer because of their proximity in time, geography, and thinking. Socrates (ca. 470–399 B.C.E.) taught Plato (ca. 428–347 B.C.E.), and Plato taught Aristotle (384–322 B.C.E.) in Athens, Greece, and all three explored the

topic of wisdom. Plato and Aristotle founded their own centers of learning—the Academy and the Lyceum, respectively. They both recorded their
teachings in writing, unlike Socrates. What is known of Socrates is primarily known through Xenophon and Aristophanes,[15] but most famously and
more thoroughly through Plato. Russell in his detailed history of Western
philosophy noted that "Plato and Aristotle were the most influential of all
philosophers, ancient, medieval, or modern, and of the two, it was Plato who
had the greatest effect upon subsequent ages."[16]

Insight to the nature of wisdom is not only revealed by what Plato and
Socrates had to say about wisdom, but also by their approach to gaining wisdom. Most of Plato's corpus consists of "dialogs"—penetrating
question-and-answer sessions around core assumptions and corresponding
beliefs designed to reveal the essence of the topic at hand, in contrast to
questions designed merely to solicit information. True of all dialogues, but
especially those of philosophers, the conversations take several trails necessary to develop precise and nuanced understanding of the phenomenon
being examined (e.g., definitions of terms, exceptions to the norm, guiding
assumptions, and sound logic, etc.). The dialogue is a trademark of philosophers and the *sine qua non* of philosophy.

Plato's dialogues provide comprehensive insight to Socrates's and Plato's
philosophy on wisdom. The *Republic*[17] is the most famous and widely read
of his corpus and consists of ten books/sections devoted to the nature of justice at the individual and societal levels. The book delves into the ends and
means of good government and the good life with corresponding insights on
wisdom.

The *Republic* opens with Socrates evaluating how several definitions
of justice are incomplete. For example, repayment of debts is just, but not
returning a sword to someone of unsound mind is more just. Socrates discussed next that justice must be more than doing good to friends and harm
to enemies, giving people what they deserve, and making enemies of friends
and vice versa. The conversation went on to establish that the just are clearly
wiser, better, abler, and happier than the unjust because of their appropriate
ends. For example, when an eye sees and the ear hears as they should, they
fulfill their respective ends. When functioning properly, without defect, they
have an excellence. Socrates demonstrated that it must be the same with the
state (formal government) and the soul (individual); they each have a proper

end and when rightly fulfilled acquire excellence. People give a nod to this notion of excellence when they judge something as "excellent" or "perfect," reflecting that the event, performance, or object in question aligns with some ideal iteration or version of what is being adjudicated.

Socrates described a just state as that in which the collective is properly coordinated so that individual members and society can thrive in mutually benefiting arrangements. In other words, Plato defined justice as the ability for people to do their "jobs"—to pursue their lot free from interference of others. In an ideal world, justice happens when things are perfectly ordered. However, this in turn begs the question, who decides a person's "job" in life—the individual or the state?

For Plato, the answer was somewhat evident in nature. Plato described three classes of people: those who produce—farmers and craftsmen (the commoners); auxiliaries (soldiers); and guardians (rulers and statesmen). According to Plato, a just society is the result of the three classes serving in their appointed roles, enabling society and individuals to survive and thrive.[18] An ideal just society consists of individuals free to perform their duties in harmony with their individual and collective destinies, fulfilling their proper roles.[19]

Book V of the *Republic* elaborated on how the guardians, as lovers of wisdom, are by default devotees to truth and goodness. Wisdom is predicated on the knowledge of what is proper or just. Socrates demonstrated that courage, temperance, and justice are companion virtues to wisdom that, when exercised together, yield justice. Wisdom discerns what is the proper (just) balance among extremes (temperance) and is useless without the courage to act accordingly. For Plato and Socrates, wisdom is the first among the virtues, discerning proper pursuits consistent with what is good, while justice is the sum of virtues. That people have "appetites"[20] is the reason there are so many admonishments to avoid vice and use reason to pursue virtue and thus experience true fulfillment. Philosophers' love for truth and acquired understanding of truth positions them to pattern their souls accordingly, with the highest virtue, thus dulling their baser appetites.

To understand justice, that which is most proper or excellent, the guardians must secure higher levels of knowledge of the true Forms, or reality as it is, different from perceptions of reality, which can be limiting and deceiving.[21] What is perceived as goodness is a shadow of the ideal form of goodness. For Plato, the world is composed of what can be sensed (the visible) and that which exists independent of thoughts, the intelligible but invisible to the senses. Plato refers to the latter as Forms—things that exist independent of the senses, such as goodness and beauty. It is in this context that justice is framed and why wisdom is necessary—a knowledge of the right ends (*sophia*) and the right means (*phronesis*) to those ends.

Plato used the poignant analogy of a captain of a ship in relation to the crew to demonstrate the utility and challenges with those who pursue *sophia*. The analogy reveals two competing types of understanding—relying on what is experienced through the senses and those that require more contemplative judgment. The captain ponders the big picture while the crew is focused on the immediate, because of their appetites and ignorance of the big picture. As a result, the crew makes fun of the captain's propensity toward the more philosophical, not even aware of its necessities and long-term benefits, and ironically considers the captain the fool. Plato in his analogy stated:

> They don't understand that a true captain must pay attention to the seasons of the year, the sky, the stars, the winds, and all that pertains to his craft, if he's really to be the ruler of a ship. And they don't believe that there is any craft that would enable him to determine how he should steer the ship, whether the others want him to or not, or any possibility of mastering this alleged craft or of practicing it at the same time as the craft of navigation. Don't you think that the true captain will be called a real stargazer, a babbler, and a good-for-nothing by those who sail in ships governed in that way?[22]

The *Republic* closes with Socrates saying that philosophy is necessary to discern the what, why, and how of a just life and society. The preceding conversations demonstrated that it is through education and the dialectic process that philosophers acquire deeper understanding of what is true, good, and beautiful. Because philosophers understand the Forms (what is ideal), the souls of people, and the ends and means of good government, all kings should be philosophers. Socrates concluded from the dialogue in the *Republic* that people reap what they sow and that the virtues promote human flourishing while the vices lead to dysfunctional endings.

In the *Republic*, wisdom is a quest for truth (i.e., the nature of reality in its purest or ideal Forms—*sophia*) and justice (i.e., function and purpose rightly aligned) accomplished by cultivating excellent understandings, dispositions, and habits (i.e., virtue). The lessons on wisdom are reiterated with additional clarity in Plato's *Laws*,[23] his last and most lengthy writing. As a result, the *Laws* "contains his latest and ripest thoughts on the subjects which he had all through his life most at his heart."[24] The *Laws* consist of twelve books and explore various ideal, practical, and technical considerations for creating a constitution for a colony of Crete, Magnesia.[25] Three elderly men—a Spartan, an Athenian, and a Cretan—are engaged in a conversation on what "laws" will best promote human flourishing (i.e., happy and virtuous citizens).[26]

During the conversation on the source and nature of laws,[27] Plato, or more specifically, the Athenian, posited a hierarchy of good within two sets of goods, the divine (i.e., virtues) and lesser human goods (i.e., health, beauty, strength, and wealth). The human goods "hang upon the divine" in which "wisdom is the chief and leader of the divine class of goods, and next follows temperance; and from the union of these two with courage springs justice, and fourth in the scale of virtue is courage."[28] The elders go on to discuss the "right education" that cultivates "harmony of the soul" by instilling virtuous habits at an early age.[29]

The dialogue in books III and IV in the *Laws* evaluated the political systems of Sparta, Athens, and Persia and discussed ideal laws for Magnesia. Book V developed the ethics and foundation for the desired good of the new colony and returned to the previous conversation on the importance of developing the soul through wise, temperate, courageous, and just character. Plato lamented that people are more prone to seek out human goods at the expense of divine goods, much to their demise. Except for Book X,[30] the remaining conversation delved into various technical and administrative considerations for creating a just and sustainable city.

What the *Republic* and *Laws* have in common are lengthy discussions on what makes societies and individuals "good"—that which fulfills their appointed purposes. A glove is good when it functionally fits the hand exactly right. A good society is just in that people are functionally able to fulfill their individual and collective purposes at ideal levels. People are good when they live up to their potential as humans, living virtuous lives. The right set of laws and education are needed to promote virtue, such that without conducive laws and education, people gravitate toward vices.

Plato provided a framework to think about the ideal. Aristotle, a pupil of Plato, tutor to Alexander the Great, and founder of his own school in Athens, elaborated upon and, in some sense, made Plato's treatment of virtue and wisdom more accessible and practical. Aristotle acknowledged that the statesperson "ought to be acquainted, not only with (1) that which is best in the abstract, but also with (2) that which is best relative to circumstances."[31] Discerning the optimal out of the many options made Aristotle more of a realist in contrast to Plato's idealism.

Aristotle's *Nicomachean Ethics* (*NE*)[32] is the most cogent of his works when it comes to understanding the nature of wisdom. The *NE* is a book devoted to happiness (flourishing) derived from human excellence (i.e., virtue), living a fully realized life. Aristotle (and Plato) used *eudaimonia*, having good *daimon* or spirit, to describe this type of happiness. Aristotle restated the thesis of *NE* in its sequel, *Politics*:[33] "For if what was said in *Ethics*[34] is true, that the happy life is the life according to virtue lived without impediment, and that virtue is a mean, then the life which is a mean, and in a mean attainable by everyone, must be the best."[35] In essence, freedom to pursue virtue (excellence) brings *eudaimonia*.[36]

The *NE* opens with a discussion on what is the highest good, positing that "the good is that at which all things aim."[37] After explaining different types of happiness (i.e., pleasure, honor, and wealth), Aristotle demonstrated in Book I that the better type of "happiness (*eudaimonia*) appears to be something complete and self-sufficient, it being an end of our actions" and "a certain sort of activity of soul in accord with virtue." Aristotle demonstrated that there are many goods, but the highest and most reasonable good for the soul is virtue and the highest and most reasonable activity of the soul is the pursuit of virtue. Again, just as a glove is good when it fits properly and serves its purpose well, life is good when it suitably fulfills its collective and individual purposes. Virtue is a thing relative to its proper work or function. A life of virtue allows people to flourish and experience a quality of fulfillment not found in lesser pursuits. For Aristotle, a life well-lived is a happy life since virtuous pursuits allow people to flourish. Virtuous pursuits are the most reasonable of all activities specific to humans.

Aristotle used the next nine books in *NE* to develop his thesis outlined in Book I. Books II through V detailed various intellectual and moral virtues. A virtue is excellence of a specific type, something that is at its peak. A most excellent performance is one that is adjudicated as flawless given its purpose and outcome. An excellent life is one that is aligned with the highest and noblest of human possibilities that makes for a complete life. In contrast, a life not living up to its potential, a life around the vices, is an incomplete life. Since moral pursuits are choices individuals make and develop through practice (what Aristotle refers to as habituation), the good life consists of noble or moral character.

Aristotle described how moral virtues are the means between deficiencies and excesses. He explains that courage is the option between cowardliness (being fearful of everything) and recklessness (being fearful of nothing), and that moderation is better than excess pleasure (licentiousness) or no pleasure (being insensible or a bore). Aristotle accordingly noted that "moderation and courage are indeed destroyed by excess and deficiency but are preserved by the mean."[38] Aristotle identified nine additional virtues or means between corresponding deficiencies and excesses to illustrate that moral virtues are practices that promote human flourishing (see Table 1.1).

Table 1.1. Aristotle's Golden Means/Virtues

Deficiency	Virtue	Excess
Cowardice	Courage	Reckless
Insensibility	Moderation	Licentiousness
Stinginess	Liberality	Prodigality
Pettiness/Parsimony	Magnificence	Crassness/Vulgarity
Timidity	Greatness of Soul	Vanity
Slothfulness	Ambition	Greed
Apathetic	Gentleness	Anger
Quarrelsome	Friendliness	Obsequious
Irony	Truthfulness	Boastful
Moroseness	Wittiness	Buffoonery
Injustice	Justice	Injustice
a. Callousness/Partiality	a. Lawful	a. Vigilantism/Partiality
b. Frivolity/Apathy	b. Equality and Equity	b. Hoarding/Narcissistic

Aristotle devoted all of Book V to the virtue of justice, noting that while it has similarities to the other virtues, it is not as simple. Aristotle believed that there cannot be too much justice, hence both its excesses and deficiencies manifest themselves as injustice. For both Plato and Aristotle, justice is a primary virtue and is doing what is fair and equitable without partiality.

Moral virtues are necessary, but not sufficient for living a good life. The intellectual virtues have as their ends (*telos*) the truth, which consists of invariable (objective) and variable (subjective) truths.[39] People need the intellectual virtues to discern their collective and individual *teloses* and corresponding golden means in accordance with correct reason. Aristotle divided the five intellectual virtues into contemplative and constructive parts of the rational soul. The contemplative truths contextualize the calculative truths.

Contemplative—focus on the ultimate ends.

1. Science (*episteme*), invariable truths that are observable and verifiable.
2. Wisdom (*sophia*), invariable universal theoretical, theological, and philosophical truths that provide ultimate understanding.
3. Intellect (*nous*), intuitive and *a priori* insights on invariable truths.

Calculative—focus on practical ends and variable truths given ultimate ends.

4. Art (*techne*), applied science (i.e., technical) that focuses on how to make things.
5. Prudence (*phronesis*), practical wisdom that allows people to discern the golden mean and right ways to act in a given situation and particulars.

Book VI was devoted to prudence. Aristotle noted that "prudence is bound up with action" and as a result, "one ought to have knowledge both of universals and particulars" if he or she is to be discerning.[40] Aristotle claimed that "all the virtues will be present when the one virtue, prudence, is present"[41] because discerning the right way to do things (*phronesis*) requires knowledge and understanding (*episteme*) of what is right, good, and beautiful (*sophia*). The right pursuit and practice of the other virtues results in *eudaimonia*. Aristotle would reiterate the relationships in his *Art of Rhetoric*, when he claimed that for speakers to be credible, they must possess *phronesis*, moral virtues, and goodwill.[42]

The last four chapters in *NE* provided additional insights on the virtuous life. Book VII highlighted the human tendency toward pleasure and warned against three practices that sabotage one's character—vice, lack of

self-restraint, and brutishness. Books VIII and IX emphasized the importance of friendship, noting that "without friends, no one would choose to
live" and "friendship holds cities together."[43] There are different types of
friendship, but the perfect or "complete friendship is the friendship of those
who are good and alike in point of virtue. For such people wish in similar
fashion for the good things for each other insofar as they are good."[44] Unfortunately, Aristotle reported that such good friendships "are likely to be rare,
since people of this sort are few."[45] Book X brought the reader back to the
opening statement in Book I, "Every art and every inquiry, and similarly
every action as well as choice is held to aim at some good"—a happy life is
the pursuit of virtue and leads to a blessed and distinctively pleasurable life.

In the *NE*, virtue (*arête*) is that which is excellent. This is the logic behind
the praise, "a most excellent job," meaning form and function were tightly
aligned. What is excellent is a function of the ultimate end and discerned
through right reasoning. A cutting knife is most excellent when it is sharp
and able to cut. An excellent butcher handles a cutting knife with ease, accuracy, and precision when fulfilling his or her function. *Sophia* is the wisdom
that determines what is the ultimate true, right, and beautiful (i.e., a cutting
knife is used for cutting). *Phronesis* is the practical wisdom that discerns the
most excellent action given the ultimate ends and the particulars of the situation (i.e., when and how to effectively use a cutting knife).[46] People are most
happy (*eudaimonia*) when they pursue the moral and intellectual virtues.

CONFUCIUS

Kong Zi (Master Kong), otherwise known as Confucius (551–479 B.C.E.), is
the Eastern counterpart to Socrates, Plato, and Aristotle. What is known about
Confucius and his teachings, much like Socrates, comes from his followers,
primarily through the *Analects*. Confucius was a native of Qufu in the province
of Shandong, China, 331 miles south of Beijing. Confucius worked as a low-
level civil servant who later became a resident teacher and philosopher.

Analects means "selected sayings." Its structure is a different type of
reading from those of Plato and Aristotle, albeit on similar topics on how to
live well in society. It is a collection of sayings compiled in variant versions
by different generations of disciples after Confucius's death. The following

summary of Tu Wei-Ming's[47] presentation, *Understanding the Confucian Analects* at the Bradley Lecture Series, highlighted the *Analects'* uniqueness and corresponding challenges when studying the text:

> Despite its place as a cornerstone of Chinese social thought, the *Analects*, said Mr. Tu, achieved only a modest reputation in the West. German philosopher Georg Hegel dismissed the text, which he believed held "no real speculative thought." Max Weber, the late-nineteenth-century German sociologist and economist, said the *Analects* praise the value of submission for the sake of established social order and lack the developed idea of the inner person revealed in the world's great philosophical works. Misread, the text seems to be no more than a random collection of proverbial utterances, a kind of ancient Chinese *Poor Richard's Almanac*. Thus, Confucian ideals have been trivialized and blurred by the popular practice of prefixing "Confucius says . . ." to so many aphorisms.
>
> Misunderstanding of the text is partially a result of the work's origins, Mr. Tu explained. Set down two generations after Confucius's death by his disciple's students, the *Analects*, written on bamboo strips, thus have no single author. Confucius's devotees selected examples of their most cherished encounters with their beloved teacher. The creation of the *Analects* was not systematic, but an act of collective memory. Those who look for a sustained argument or unified tract, therefore, are invariably disappointed.[48]

In his translation of and commentary on the *Analects*, Edward Slingerland noted that:

> The *Analects* is not a "book" in the sense that most modern Westerners usually understand a book—that is a coherent argument or story. . . . It is instead a record—somewhat haphazardly collected and edited together at an unknown point in history—a dynamic process of teaching, and most likely was only committed to writing many years after the primary touchstone of the process, the Master Confucius, had passed away. It probably represents an attempt by later students and followers to keep alive the memory of his teaching, which had been conveyed both verbally and by personal example.[49]

Since the *Analects* is not a traditional book, it must be read in a different way. As a result of its dynamic construction over time, Slingerland observed that:

Many, if not most, of the passages are quite cryptic, and this may be at least partially intentional. . . . As we see throughout the text, Confucius' comments are often intended to elicit responses from his disciples, which are then corrected or commented upon by the Master. Therefore, these "ordered sayings" of Confucius were originally embedded in a conversational context within which their meaning could gradually be extracted.[50]

Regardless of its interpretive challenges, the *Analects* remain a foundational and representative text in the Chinese tradition. Leys noted in his translation of the *Analects* that "no book in the entire history of the world has exerted, over a longer period of time, a greater influence on a larger number of people than this slim little volume."[51] At one point "the *Analects* became required to pass 'examination,' the mandatory test for entry into the civil service of ancient China, Japan, Korea, and Vietnam."[52]

The *Analects* consists of twenty groupings, small books with sayings attributed to the Master. The sayings get to the heart of ethics, how people should conduct themselves, especially public officials. A major theme in the *Analects* is captured in 1.14: "The gentleman [noble one] is not motivated by the desire for a full belly or a comfortable abode. He is simply scrupulous in behavior and careful in speech, drawing near to those who possess the Way in order to be set straight by them. Surely this and nothing else is what it means to love learning."[53]

The Way (*dao*) refers to a moral path. As indicated in 1.14, it is a different path, not primarily motivated by externalities like food and comfort. Its fruit is careful speech and conduct. It is acquired by being yoked to like-minded individuals who model the Way. The sixteen passages in Book One teach that peoples' deportment in the form of respect, duty, and truth matter above all other things and are the signs that learning has happened. Learning the Way is about proper conduct, not limited to academic knowledge.

Book Two opens with the Master stating, "One who rules the Power of Virtue (*de*) is analogous to the Pole Star: It simply remains in its place and receives homage of the myriad lesser stars" (2.1). Confucius posited later in 2.3 and 2.19 that the common people should be guided by Virtue rather than force so that they will govern themselves to do good. Confucius is noting that moral worthiness is an endearing influence, more powerful than other types of power, that is achieved by embracing the Way.[54]

The younger person who resolves to embrace the Way is better positioned to die without regret—"Having in the morning heard the Way was being put into practice, I could die that evening without regret" (4.8). Confucius noted in 2.4 that: "At fifteen I set my mind upon learning; at thirty, I took my place in society; at forty, I became free of doubts; at fifty, I understood Heaven's Mandate; at sixty, my ear was attuned; and at seventy, I could follow my heart's desires without overstepping the bounds of propriety."

The value of learning is underscored in 2.10: "Both keeping the past teachings alive and understanding the present—someone who is able to do this is worthy of being a teacher." In 2.15, "If you learn without thinking about what you have learned, you will be lost. If you think without learning, however, you will fall into danger." Confucius observed that it was his love for learning that set him apart (5.28).

Confucius lamented in Book Three that the Way to Virtue is the less-traveled path. Portions of the recorded dialogue critiqued some who violated honored traditions and wandered off the moral path. Book Three provided a prelude to Confucius's version of the doctrine of the mean outlined in Book Six, paralleling the logic of Aristotle's concept of prudence as discerning the golden mean. Confucius noted that "When it comes to ritual, it is better to be spare [frugal] than extravagant. When it comes to mourning, it is better to be excessively sorrowful than fastidious [ease]" (3.4). Depending on the context, some virtues are better than others (i.e., it's okay to be excessive with mourning, but not with rituals). Book Three concluded with the Master saddened at the prospect that, "Someone who lacks magnanimity when occupying high office, who is not respectful when performing ritual, and who remains unmoved by sorrow when overseeing mourning rites—how could I bear to look upon such a person?" (3.26).

Book Four is devoted to goodness and wisdom and that one cannot have the latter without the former. The opening passage noted that "To live in the neighborhood [company] of the Good (ren) is fine. If one does not choose to dwell among those who are Good, how will one obtain wisdom (zhi)?" (4.1).[55] Slingerland noted that "Goodness refers to the highest virtue of Confucian virtues . . . the overarching virtue of being a perfected human being, which includes such qualities as empathetic understanding (shu) and benevolence (hui)."[56] Goodness is a corequisite to wisdom and acquired in part by being yoked to good people. According to Confucius, the petty person cherishes material things and seeks favor while the noble person cherishes virtue through discipline (4.11) and that the virtuous never lack true friends (4.25).

Books Five and Six provide examples of virtuous thought and acts displayed by historical and contemporary figures. For example, in 5.16, the Master said of Zichan, "Of the virtues that constitute the Way of the gentleman, he possessed four: in the way he conducted himself, he displayed reverence; in the way he served his superiors, he displayed respect; in the way he cared for common people, he displayed benevolence; and in the way he employed the people, he displayed rightness."

It is in Book Six that Confucius provided some direct instruction on the nature of wisdom. As in Book Three, Confucius pondered in 6.17 why people do not pursue the Way, acknowledging throughout the *Analects* that is the more difficult path that requires superior understanding (6.18–22). When asked about wisdom in public administration, the Master noted in 6.22–23:

> Working to ensure social harmony among the common people, respecting the ghosts and spirits while keeping them at a distance—this might be called wisdom. . . . One who is Good sees his first priority the hardship of self-cultivation, and only after thinks about results or rewards. Yes, this is what we might call Goodness. . . . The wise take joy in the rivers, while the Good takes joy in mountains. The wise are active, while the Good are still. The wise are joyful, while the Good are long-lived.

Confucius noted that wisdom is about action that flows from the perennial truths associated with Goodness acquired by arduous and altruistic self-cultivation. Just a few passages earlier (6.18) and later (6.29), Confucius referenced the doctrine of the mean, as if channeling Aristotle's *NE*. In 6.29, "Acquiring Virtue by applying the mean—is this not the best? And yet among the common people few are able to practice this virtue for long." This nuance to wisdom is captured in 9.29, "The wise (*zhi*) are not confused, the Good (*ren*) do not worry, and the courageous (*yong*) do not fear." In other words, the wise are discerning, free from perplexities. Like Aristotle, Confucius's grouping of the *zhi*, *ren*, and *yong* reveals that doing good requires wisdom and courage.

Reminiscent of the dialogue between Phaedrus and Socrates referenced in the Preface, Confucius reserved the title of sage (*sheng ren*) for the just and benevolent rulers. He claimed that he himself was not qualified for the title; it was better reserved for those who judiciously attended to the needs of the masses, enabling the masses to be successful (6.29), even though he worked hard for it (7.34, 9.8, 14.28).

Timothy Connolly unpacked three levels of moral achievement identified in the *Analects*, of which the sage is the highest and highlights an interesting tension between the three.

The three levels of moral achievement that appear most prominently in the *Analects*—scholar-official (*shi*), gentleman, and sage—suggest a rough course of progress expected of Confucius' students. At the initial stage of scholar-official, a student has made an act of commitment (*zhi*) to the pursuit of the Confucian way (*dao*). The ability to maintain this commitment in the face of hardship and temptation is a central feature of the scholar-official, and his struggle is said to terminate only in death. At a higher level than the scholar-official is the gentleman, [noble person] or *junzi*. Whereas the scholar-official may have noticeable flaws, the *junzi* does not act contrary to goodness (*ren*) for the time of one meal; his lack of faults makes him free from any worry or fear. Yet even so, *the junzi* is said to "stand in awe of the teachings of the sages." The most likely candidates for the latter title in the *Analects* are the ancient kings Yao, Shun, and Yu—rulers capable of "extending [their] benevolence to the common people and bringing succor to the multitudes."

While sagehood is clearly the highest level of achievement, the *Analects* presents us with a puzzle regarding its status. On the one hand, it is the teachings of the sage-kings which Confucius claims to be transmitting, and the text presents the conduct of the ancient sage-kings as a guide for students' moral development and their behavior in leadership roles. Yet on the other hand, as Rodney Taylor points out, there appears to be "no attempt to suggest that one can reach the state of sagehood." With this ambivalent treatment of sagehood, we are left without a clear notion of how good Confucius thinks we should try to be.[57]

Connolly solved the puzzle in part when he stated that:

Confucius recognizes the danger of ideals that push us beyond our limits. And he is similarly cognizant of human limitations, including the limitations of his own devoted followers. But his concern for human limitation is balanced out by the belief that we are capable of transcending our deficiencies through accumulated effort spread out over a lifetime. It is this emphasis on human development that distinguishes the early Confucian conception of sagehood. We should not try to become sages all at once, but we nonetheless should try.[58]

Book Seven reiterated principles previously identified, such as 7.6, "Set your heart upon the Way, rely upon Virtue, lean upon Goodness, and explore widely in your cultivation of the arts." As in 1.6 and 3.8, the cultural arts were a means to cultivate an aesthetical understanding of the Way. Book Eight is similar to Books Five and Six, filled with examples of good and bad judgments. Book Nine highlighted additional virtues such as focus, sincerity, perseverance, and self-cultivation as parts of the Way. Slingerland described Book Ten as "a sort of capstone,"[59] as it highlights Confucius's effortless embodiment of the Way in various situations.

Books Eleven and Twelve provided additional commentary of wisdom from Confucius's disciples with examples of doing/being good at the individual, familial, and public-service levels (e.g., respect, proper comportment, slowness to speak, duty, etc.). The passage in 12.10 captured the essence, "Make it your guiding principle to be dutiful and trustworthy, and always move in the direction of what is right. This is what it means to accumulate Virtue." The accumulation of Virtue is in part predicated on good learning and prevents people from wrongdoing—"Someone broadly learned with regard to culture, and whose conduct is restrained by rites, can be counted on to not go astray" (12.15, also 6.27).

Books Thirteen and Fourteen reiterated and demonstrated that virtue is the best way to govern. Book Fifteen is filled with an assortment of useful aphorisms and instructions for living a noble/virtuous life. It contrasts the thoughts and actions of petty individuals and functionaries (13.20) with those of more noble individuals and leaders. It provides perspective to rightly judge character since associates determine if individuals and governments practice virtue, given that character is to be valued over other considerations (14.33). Confucius noted that a complete person is wise, free from desire, courageous, and that such completeness is acquired by "means of ritual and music" (14.12). Book 14, passage 28, repeated what was stated in 9.29, highlighting the importance of virtue ethics: "The Good do not worry, the wise are not confused, and the courageous do not fear." Similar to Aristotle, goodness without wisdom and courage is impotent, courage without goodness and wisdom is dangerous, and wisdom without goodness and courage is useless.

Books Sixteen through Twenty take on a different tenor and structure than the preceding books, while retaining similar themes and content. For example, Confucius is referred to as Kongzi in the text rather than "The Master," and the individual passages are longer and not as cohesive in thought, reflecting that the collection was a later stratum.[60] Book Seventeen highlighted the problem of hypocrisy. Books Eighteen and Nineteen cited examples and counterexamples of different people, as foils to teach the Way. Book Twenty has three passages that contain an assortment of last-minute advice not necessarily addressed in the first nineteen books. The rushed and abrupt conclusion to the *Analects* suggests that there is not enough time or space to address every contingency associated with navigating the Way, leaving it to the reader to develop guidelines or principles from the preceding books, accordingly.

This brief walk through the *Analects* reveals that life is filled with choices and that some pursuits are better than others. Confucius argued that the virtuous path is better and results in a level of cultivated discernment to understand and do what is right (appropriate), for "the gentleman [noble one] admires rightness above all" (17.23). Slingerland described this rightness (*yi*) as "a kind of cultivated sense of what is right and morally proper" and "rightful duty."[61] The Chinese moral philosopher Jiyuan Yu described the concept as "what is fitting" or "what is appropriate"[62] as being like Aristotle's concept of *eudaimonia*. The *Analects*, similar to *NE*, argued that the virtuous person does what is morally appropriate in a given situation governed by the knowledge of the Way, and that without virtue, a person is limited in his or her ability to know and do what is ultimately appropriate.

Yu demonstrated that *yi* [appropriate, right] in the *Analects* is closely associated with wisdom (*zhi*). Wisdom involves discerning what is appropriate according to desired outcomes. While in the *Analects*, wisdom is something that "can be shared by both virtuous and non-virtuous persons," it is primarily associated with discerning good,[63] akin to Aristotle's treatment of wisdom as an intellectual virtue. Slingerland described *zhi* (wisdom) in the *Analects* as an "important virtue that seems to involve cognitive understanding of the

Way, as well as an ability to perceive situations and judge the characters of others."[64] In the *Analects*, wisdom is closely connected to the Way—discerning the moral path. It is inextricably tied to being and doing good (*ren*), embodying a set of virtues (e.g., benevolence, duty, respect, etc.) acquired through knowledge, practice, and aesthetical pursuits like music and culture. Wisdom allows one to perceive accurately, without perplexities. It is an enlightened understanding of the Way that results in good actions among competing options.

AL-FARABI, AVICENNA, AND AVERROES

The Golden Age of Islam (ca. 786–1258) yielded discoveries and advancements in agriculture, astronomy, chemistry, engineering, geography, math, medicine, music, optics, philosophy, and science.[65] Muslims of that time demonstrated a commitment to preserve, translate, and study the intellectual traditions situated in their expanding empire. Ali Haj Mohammed, in "Historical Background of Arab Achievements in the Islamic Golden Age," noted:

> As Muslims of the Islamic Empire expanded their empire, they were opened to ideas and customs of the people they conquered. Along with those ideas and customs were those from Greece, Rome and Asia—which influenced and became part of the Muslim culture. Each conquered civilization had its own importance to the development of the Islamic Empire and how it made major advancements.[66]

Libraries from this time in Baghdad (called the House of Wisdom), Cairo, Cordoba, and Tripoli archived and translated manuscripts from the known world and served as places for scholars to convene and conduct research. These esteemed intellectual centers with vast holdings were responsible for synthesizing accumulated knowledge and fostering new knowledge.[67]

Just as the Greeks had their three prominent philosophers that shaped Western civilization, the Golden Age of Islam had three: Al-Farabi (ca. 870–950), Avicenna (ca. 980–1037), and Averroes (1126–1198). These Muslim philosophers connected science and philosophy with theology, treating them as complementary forms of knowledge of the truth, contrary to the prevailing opinion of many who thought such integration was an assault to Islam. Although they were original thinkers and prolific writers on a wide array of topics, they embraced Plato's and Aristotle's corpora to inform their philosophical assumptions and writings,[68] earning the appellation of "Aristotle's children."[69]

Al-Farabi, nicknamed the "Second Teacher"[70] after Aristotle, had an encyclopedic mind and was a prolific scholar writing on logic, physics, astronomy, music, and politics. He argued that logic is a universal grammar that "provides the rules for correct reasoning in all languages."[71] That he admired Plato and Aristotle is evident by several of his books: *Opinions of the Inhabitants of the Virtuous City* (with a similar theme and message as found in Plato's *Republic*), the *Philosophy of Plato and Aristotle*, and *Compendium of the Laws*, the *Philosophy of Aristotle*, and the *Attainment of Happiness* (which uses Aristotle's construct of *eudaimonia*). Fakhry, in his comprehensive survey of Islamic philosophy, stated:

> Al-Farabi's contribution in physics, metaphysics, and politics, as well as in logic, entitles him to a position of undoubted preeminence among the philosophers of Islam. He is particularly commended by one of his earliest historiographers for his masterly exposition of the philosophies of Plato and Aristotle. These two works, together with his *Enumeration of the Sciences*, are the most comprehensive general introduction to Aristotelianism and Platonism in Arabic, and they far surpass in quality and completeness any parallel works of that period.[72]

The second notable Islamic philosopher, Avicenna (Ibn Sina), was a savant. He had memorized the Quran by the age of ten, and he had mastered Euclid's *Elements* and Aristotle's *Physics* and *Metaphysics* on his own before practicing medicine by the time he was sixteen. At the age of seventeen, he wrote *Treatise on the Soul in the Manner of Summary*.[73] He was an accomplished scientist and philosopher and a prolific scholar in medicine, philosophy, art, and astronomy. Avicenna's two most important works were *The Book of Healing* and *The Canon of Medicine*. The first is a scientific encyclopedia covering logic, natural sciences, psychology, geometry, astronomy, arithmetic, and music. The second is considered the "most famous single book in the history of medicine."[74]

Avicenna was considered the "greatest and most influential philosopher of the Islamic world," who "is without doubt the one thinker who is most responsible for integrating and, even more significantly, naturalizing classical Greek philosophical and medical thought into Islamic intellectual life."[75] David Burrell observed in his commentary on Avicenna that "there can be little doubt that Avicenna wanted Hellenic philosophy to assist in the articulation of his Muslim faith" and described him as the "prolific adapter of Aristotle, accomplished in logic, who fairly defined Islamic *falasifa* (an Arabic transliteration of 'philosophy')" . . . "as well as the composer of allegories intended to lead the inquiring intellect to the very source of wisdom in the uncreated One."[76]

Averroes (Ibn Rushd) of Cordoba, Spain, was the only Muslim philosopher included in the famed *School of Athens* painted by Raphael. Averroes wrote "more than 100 works on theology, jurisprudence, philosophy, astronomy, and medicine."[77] Fakhry remarked that:

the philosophical output of Ibn Rushd was as voluminous and varied as that of any of the greater philosophers of the East. Two characteristic features set his work apart from that of the two Eastern masters—Al-Farabi and Ibn Sina, his only two equals in the world of Islam: his meticulousness in commenting on the texts of Aristotle and his conscientiousness in grappling with the perennial question of the relation of philosophy with dogma.[78]

Averroes was tasked by his prince to produce an extensive series of commentaries on Aristotle's corpus, thus earning the nickname "'The Commentator' by the Christian West."[79] While not necessarily embraced by his fellow Muslims, his reception in the West elevated his status as the "scholar who gave us modern philosophy."[80]

Just a few years after his [Averroes's] death in Marrakesh, the great universities of Europe began operation, most notably in Paris and Oxford. Unlike the strictly religious character of their nearest Islamic counterparts, these European universities were, from the start, thoroughly secular in their undergraduate curricula. The usual course of studies ran through subjects such as logic, metaphysics, ethics, and natural science—in short, they were exposed to all the various parts of philosophy. Students might go on to the advanced study of medicine, law, or theology, but each of those disciplines were taken to have their foundation in philosophy. By the middle of the thirteenth century, that philosophical curriculum had become thoroughly Aristotelian, and the great guide to Aristotle was none other than Averroes, who became known in the Latin West as simply "the Commentator." His various paraphrases and commentaries on the Aristotelian corpus were studied wherever Aristotle was studied, and this remained the case all the way into the modern era. Even though, by the end of the Middle Ages, there were countless Christian commentaries on the Aristotelian corpus, it was still the writings of Averroes that were most likely to be found alongside early printed editions of Aristotle's work.[81]

In his commentary on Averroes, Richard Taylor wrote:

Averroes' deep admiration for the philosophical works of Aristotle caused him to work hard to explain and solve philosophical problems from Greek thought that were still vital and current in his medieval Islamic philosophical context. Issues in Aristotelian epistemology and metaphysics continue to attract the interest of philosophers and historians of philosophy today; in light of that modern scholars would be well served to make the most of the insights of Averroes in his commentaries and other philosophical works. But it is in the area of modern philosophy of religion that the thought of Averroes can be seen to have valuable insights to offer today, both to his co-religionists and to other philosophers and theologians. Averroes argued forcefully about the nature and interpretation of texts, in particular against naive scriptural literalism as well as against insufficiently founded religious presumptions. He strived to show that the principle 'Truth does not contradict truth but rather is consistent with it and bears witness to it' entails that reason and religion must ultimately be one and without contradiction, and that philosophy has a fundamentally important role to play in religion.[82]

Al-Farabi, Avicenna, and Averroes provided three important clues to the nature of wisdom useful for this chapter. They implicitly endorsed their Greek counterparts' notions of wisdom in their nuanced commentaries on Plato and Aristotle. For all practical purposes, the nature of wisdom in the Golden Age of Islam mirrored what Aristotle and Plato taught. For this reason, this primer did not walk through representative writings from the three Muslim philosophers, since their thoughts on the subject relied heavily on the teachings of Plato and Aristotle. The second clue on the nature of wisdom comes from what facilitated the rise of the Golden Age of Islam: the desire to embrace knowledge from multiple sources. The quest for knowledge that defined this era of Islam cultivated understanding, a prerequisite for new knowledge and wisdom. The third and maybe more important contribution was establishing a positive relationship between philosophy and theology. Philosophy and theology are not only companions in the search for truth, but they are also necessary to each other. Philosophy leads to theology, and theology requires philosophy. Theology helps identify Aristotle's "unmoved mover" and Plato's Forms, while philosophy sharpens theology's conclusions and language.

Averroes, like Avicenna and Al-Farabi, established that science (empiricism), philosophy, and theology are necessary to know truth, and as a result are compatible, while also acknowledging that theology is the ultimate source and value of knowing. They provided the logic for the dictum that "philosophy was the handmaiden of theology."[83]

CONCLUSION

Just as one does not need to eat a whole cake to appreciate the fullness of its taste, one does not need to read every philosopher to get a sense of the nature of wisdom in the philosophical tradition. Boethius, Socrates, Plato, Aristotle, and Confucius's perspectives on wisdom, and Al-Farabi, Avicenna, and Averroes's endorsement of Plato and Aristotle, provide a representative sense of the nature of wisdom, especially since they appear to be saying similar things.

The philosophers treat wisdom primarily as an intellectual virtue with two overlapping types of elevated understandings. *Sophia* is the contemplative wisdom that concerns itself with discerning the right *teloses* based upon an accurate understanding of truth (Forms). *Phronesis* is more calculative and focuses on right means given the cherished and better ends. *Sophia* tends to deal with universals and the ideal while *phronesis* deals with the particulars (i.e., the golden means) and the more practical. It is difficult to practice *phronesis* without some level of *sophia*. Likewise, *sophia* is relatively useless without *phronesis*. Hence, wisdom is a combination of the two. While Plato, Aristotle, and Confucius might debate what *teloses* exist and which are the better or should take priority in given situations (i.e., the content of wisdom), they have in common that wisdom is ultimately about the "highest goods" and "most excellent" understandings and practices.

Wisdom is also considered a moral virtue since it is discerning which ends and means are the best ones relative to the many good options, at both the universal and the practical levels. Why pursue wisdom if not to be virtuous? Wisdom leads to virtuous thinking and doing, and vice versa. Wisdom makes the other virtues possible, and the other virtues make wisdom necessary. Wisdom without courage is impotent, and courage without wisdom is reckless. Wisdom without wit is cumbersome, while wit without wisdom is distracting. Wisdom without temperance is wearisome, and temperance without wisdom is meaningless.

Wisdom is a nuanced understanding about the nature of reality (contemplative), and the aligning of thoughts, dispositions, and habits and practices to the more meaningful patterns or storylines in particular situations (calculative). Wisdom is the honest pursuit of truth, predicated on advanced levels of knowledge and understanding of the nature of reality that results in enlightened judgments about what is true, good, and beautiful. Wisdom leads to meaningful lives and promotes human flourishing. It recognizes that lesser pursuits and habits, like the vices, are distractions and/or detours that diminish, if not degrade, flourishing. The philosophers also demonstrated that wisdom is acquired through candid and honest dialectic inquiry. Socrates immortalized this sentiment in his declaration that "the life which is unexamined is not worth living."[84]

REFLECTION AND DISCUSSION QUESTIONS

1. What does Lady Philosophy in Boethius suggest is the ultimate path to meaning given the fickle nature of fate?
2. What are the false comforts identified by Lady Philosophy and why do they so deceive and deprive people of ultimate fulfillment?
3. What does Boethius's description of Lady Philosophy suggest about the nature of wisdom and possibly how the wise present themselves?

4. How might a person's deportment (their demeanor, behaviors, and manners) be a manifestation of wisdom, according to Boethius, Aristotle, and Confucius?
5. What is happiness, according to Plato and Aristotle?
6. What is the relationship between virtue, vice, and the "good" and happy life, according to Plato and Aristotle?
7. According to Plato, why should leaders be philosophers?
8. What is the golden mean, according to Aristotle and Confucius, and what is its relationship to wisdom?
9. What is the relationship between broad learning, cultural intelligence, music, and wisdom, according to Confucius?
10. How did the Golden Age of Islam and Al-Farabi, Avicenna, and Averroes contribute to the nature of wisdom?

2

THEOLOGICAL PERSPECTIVES ON WISDOM

Theology is the study (*ology*) of god (*theos*). *Theology* refers to the systematic study of doctrines, beliefs, and practices in relationship to the divine. While philosophy also involves the study of beliefs and practices, questions and conclusions are restricted to what is rationally defensible based on logical inferences. Theology assumes that the divine exists and involves faith seeking understanding. Philosophy may or may not assume the divine and involves reason seeking understanding. While religion deals with similar areas as philosophy and theology, religion tends to focus more on the practices and duties of one's faith. Theology tends to "designate a higher level of reflection to which the claims of a particular religion may possibly be subjected."[1] Theologians can be religious or non-religious, and religious people can be theologians or non-theologians.

A prolific theological scholar, Dr. Mark Worthing highlighted the distinction between theology and other areas of study when he wrote that "theology was viewed as wisdom because it dealt with things eternal while the other disciplines were viewed as science because they dealt with things temporal."[2] In outlining the history of thinking, he described how theology "quickly assumed the status within the medieval university of 'Queen of the Sciences.'"[3]

It is interesting to note that the Greek word for *philosophy* occurs only once in the New Testament,[4] and it is a relatively pejorative reference to a system of thought based upon "the tradition of man, according to the principles of the world" (Col. 2:8). While wisdom from the philosopher is concerned with living a good life defined by purpose (i.e., *eudaimonia*), theology is about living life well according to revealed truth claims about the nature of god(s) and peoples' relationship to god(s). Theologician Dr. Chris Morgan astutely observed in his commentary on the book of James that "for all practical purposes, religion and wisdom go hand-in-hand" and posited "that the major aim of theology is wisdom" and that "wisdom at its core is theological."[5] While the theological perspective on wisdom can be foreign to some philosophers and empiricists who dismiss the existence of the supernatural, it does provide relevant insights on the nature of wisdom akin to the philosophical and empirical perspectives of wisdom described in chapters 1 and 3, respectively.

In most theological traditions, it is understood that there are two sources of revelation for people to discover and know the divine. The first source is general revelation and encompasses all of nature. The second source is special revelation, usually in the form of a sacred text. The reliance on special revelation and/or enlightened texts to better understand the nature of reality is a fascinating element about most world religions. Hindus have the Vedas (knowledge). Buddhists have the Sutras. Jews have the TaNaK.[6] Muslims have the Quran. Christians have the Bible (the TaNaK and the New Testament). Even some offshoots of Christianity appeal to additional revelation beyond the Bible for the basis of their beliefs. For example, the Latter-Day Saints of Jesus Christ have the Book of Mormon, while the Christian Scientists have the authoritative writings of Mary Baker Eddy.

Special revelation is required because general revelation discloses only so much about the nature of reality. General revelation deals with those truths in the natural world and is accessible to all people. For example, the various academic disciplines, such as anthropology, biology, chemistry, philosophy, psychology, and physics, are systematic approaches to the study of reality in the natural and social worlds. In contrast, theology is the systematic study of both the natural and supernatural worlds based upon truths made accessible by supernatural, or "special," means.

The Judeo-Christian tradition has an explicit theology regarding general and special revelation. The Bible describes how natural revelation provides evidence of a holy and loving God and exhorts people to search for him.

Judeo-Christian theology shows that special revelation picks up where general revelation leaves off. The first six verses of Psalm 19 describe how nature reveals an awesome Creator. The psalm opens with: "The heavens are telling of the glory of God; and their expanse is declaring the work of His hands. Day to day pours forth speech, and night to night reveals knowledge" (Psalm 19:1–2). The reader of Psalm 19 is encouraged to reflect on the beauty and complexity of the world (i.e., natural revelation). Such reflection allows the reader to experience the momentum of the passage, so that by the time he or she gets to the end of verse 6, there is a longing to know more about this Creator. The subsequent verses direct the reader to special revelation, in this case the Torah (the first five books of the TaNaK/Bible). Psalm 19:7–13 reveals that meditation and observance of the Torah are the means to discern the identity of the Creator. Students of the Torah learn that God is personal, holy, loving, and forgiving. Psalm 19 ends by highlighting an appropriate response to a personal relationship with the God of the Bible: "Let the words of my mouth and the meditation of my heart be acceptable in Your sight, O Lord, my rock and my Redeemer" (Psalm 19:14). Nature provides people with a glimpse of a powerful and caring God and directs them to special revelation (Psalm 19:1–6). As a result of studying the Bible, people discover that they are invited into a redeemed relationship with a holy and loving God (Psalm 19:7–13), resulting in a transformed life (Psalm 19:14). In short, general revelation points to God, and special revelation describes God in detail.

The encouraging explicit and implicit message from the major theological texts is that wisdom is attainable. For example, Proverbs 1:20 reveals that wisdom shouts in the street and in the public square. The book of Proverbs implores young hearts and minds to make their ears attentive to wisdom and search for her "as for hidden treasure" (Proverbs 2:1–4).[7] The Vedas, Sanskrit for "knowledge," conveys to the pupil that it contains sacred knowledge to live wisely. The word *Quran* is Arabic for "recite." By reciting Allah's message, Muslims know how to obey, or submit to Allah, to live good lives. The etymology of the word *Bible* is derived from the koine Greek word for "book." In the Christian tradition, the holy "book" is believed to be "inspired by God and profitable for teaching, for reproof, for correction, and for training in righteousness; so that the man of God may be adequate, equipped for every good work" (2 Timothy 3:16–17). All religious texts claim to be the source of truth for people to know the right way to live, given the nature of God as "revealed" in their respective texts.[8] This is a first clue to the nature of wisdom in the theological tradition. It involves deriving beliefs, values, virtues, and habits from a transcendent authority on the nature of both temporal and eternal realities.

The study of the major religious texts of Judaism, Christianity, Islam, and Hinduism provide relevant insights on the nature of wisdom, although the content of the wisdom differs. While other theological texts exist and are worthy of study for their insights on the nature of wisdom, time and space here do not allow for a comprehensive comparative analysis. It is reasonable to infer that the common elements on the nature of wisdom portrayed in the Bible (Judaism and Christianity), the Quran (Islam), and the Vedas (Hinduism) are also found in other faith texts and will suffice to provide a representative understanding of wisdom in the theological traditions. As already stated, but necessary to underscore, this chapter is evaluating the nature of wisdom as revealed by the texts of four world religions. This chapter is not evaluating the content of such wisdom or the veracity of the major religions. As stated in the preface, while content and structure are related, just as different sizes and styles of houses share similar architectural and structural features, the theological texts share similar, yet different, teachings on wisdom.[9]

THE BIBLE—THE JUDAIC AND CHRISTIAN NATURE OF WISDOM

The Bible consists of the Hebrew Scriptures (i.e., the TaNaK) and the New Testament. It provides insights to the nature of wisdom from both the Jewish and Christian faith traditions. The treatment of wisdom in the Bible falls into two categories. The first category is the wisdom genre. The Wisdom Books of the Bible include Job, Proverbs, Ecclesiastes, Song of Solomon, and James and share distinctive traits parallel to the wisdom literature of the Ancient Near East.[10] Wisdom literature relies on an earthbound perspective as the reference point to make meaningful and practical conclusions about life. The authors condense the knowledge from observed consistencies and patterns found in the world and human interactions into maxims and instructions. A dominant motif in the wisdom literature is the law of the harvest— people reap what they sow. A second and related motif is that certain sets of

THEOLOGICAL PERSPECTIVES ON WISDOM

thoughts and habits are better than others—cultivating virtues (the way of the wise) is better than pursuing vices (the way of the fools).

The book of Proverbs is mostly about navigating life under relatively normal circumstances. Conversely, the book of Job reveals insights for those life experiences outside of the norm, when life goes tragically wrong, especially for "good" people. Ecclesiastes imparts existential insights to the meaning of life given its brevity and, at times, the appearance of a lack of fairness and order. The book of James provides practical perspectives for a pure and undefiled religion that begins with the reminder that God generously provides wisdom to the believers who ask accordingly (James 1:5). The Song of Solomon celebrates the gift of intimate love.

That the Bible has a corpus of books and a genre devoted to wisdom does not mean that the other books in the Bible do not speak to wisdom. The remaining books in the Bible have much to say about wisdom. For example, in the book of Ephesians, the apostle Paul spent the first three chapters teaching theology about God's love, grace, and mercy toward his children of faith. He then entreated believers "to walk in the manner worthy of the calling with which you have been called" (Eph. 4:1). Paul used the next three chapters to provide principles for godly living. Paul admonished the believers to walk "not as unwise [asophia] men, but as wise [sophia], making the most of their days" (Eph. 5:15).

The primary Hebrew word for wisdom in the TaNaK is derived from the verbal root *chakam* (חָכַם). The primary Greek words for wisdom in the New Testament are *sophia* (σοφία) and *phronesis* (φρόνησις). Wisdom is often juxtaposed with foolishness. In the book of Proverbs, the fool was the counterexample to the wise. Proverbs 1:7 states that "fools despise wisdom and instruction." In Proverbs 10:1, "a wise son makes his father glad, but a foolish son is a grief to his mother." Solomon, in Ecclesiastes 7:5, observed that "it is better to listen to the rebuke of a wise man than for one to listen to the song of fools." In Matthew 7:24–27, at the conclusion of the Sermon on the Mount, Jesus stated:

> Therefore everyone who hears these words of Mine and acts on them, may be compared to a wise [*phronesis*] man who built his house on the rock. And the rain fell, and the floods came, and the winds blew and slammed against that house; and yet it did not fall, for it had been founded on the rock. Everyone

who hears these words of Mine and does not act on them, will be like a foolish man who built his house on the sand. The rain fell, and the floods came, and the winds blew and slammed against that house; and it fell and great was its fall.

THE HEBREW BIBLE

By the time the major corpus of the wisdom literature in the Hebrew tradition was developed, during the reign of Kings David and Solomon (1020–940 B.C.E.), the Hebrews already had a theological understanding of wisdom. Their covenantal relationship with God and instructions on how to live a holy life were recorded in the Torah, the first five books of the Hebrew Bible.

The book of Genesis explains how and why God established a covenantal relationship with his redeemed people. God promised Abraham, the first patriarch of the Jewish nation, a land and a multitude of descendants who would be a blessing to the rest of the world (Gen. 12:1–3; 15:1–21; 17:1–22). The narrative in Genesis articulates God's plan for His creation and provides the theological foundation for truths and doctrines that appear in the subsequent books of the Bible, including the New Testament.

The book of Exodus records how the Jewish nation "increased greatly, and multiplied, and became exceedingly mighty" in the land of Egypt (Exod. 1:7). In this regard, Egypt was an incubator for an emerging nation to take on an identity without the threat of external conflict. After several hundred years of unhindered growth, the number of Israelites and their prosperity triggered the Egyptians' insecurities, and the Egyptian rulers decided to enslave the Israelites. This was the preordained impetus for God to relocate his people to the land promised to Abraham in Genesis. God raised up Moses to lead Israel's en masse departure from Egypt. As they were en route to the Promised Land, God reminded them that they were to be a holy people (Exod. 19:6) and provided them the Ten Commandments to codify his expectations.

The book of Leviticus, often referred to as the Book of Laws, provides specific instructions and guidelines for Israel to celebrate and maintain a special covenantal relationship with a holy God and to live set apart from other nations. In Leviticus 18:1–5:

34

The Lord spoke to Moses, saying, "Speak to the sons of Israel and say to them, 'I am the LORD your God. You shall not do what is done in the land of Egypt where you lived, nor are you to do what is done in the land of Canaan where I am bringing you; you shall not walk in their statutes. You are to perform My judgments and keep My statutes, to live in accord with them; I am the LORD your God. So you shall keep My statutes and My judgments, by which a man may live if he does them; I am the LORD.'"

While many sections of Leviticus read strangely to the uninitiated reader, there is a structure and cohesiveness that reveals a caring, holy, and personal God who has a special purpose and high expectations for his people and ambassadors to other nations.

The book of Numbers, so named because of its detailed census accounts,[11] highlights the consequences of faith and disbelief. As the faith community of Israel entered the land flowing with milk and honey, they feared the inhabitants were too strong for them to conquer. The generation of people who experienced God's miraculous deliverance from Egypt and provisions in the desert expressed unbelief, and as result God decreed that their children, not them, would enter the Promised Land (Numbers 11 and 12). The remainder of the book documents the transition to the next generation of Israelites and corresponding lessons on faith and obedience.

The book of Deuteronomy, the fifth book of the Torah, consists of a series of sermons to the new generation. The Israelites are reminded multiple times throughout the text to "be careful." The new and subsequent generations were instructed to be careful to keep the commandments, to teach their children God's heart, and to remember His statutes. The heart of Jewish theology in the Torah is captured in Deuteronomy 6:4–9, which is the guiding principle for Old Testament wisdom:

Hear, O Israel! The LORD is our God, the LORD is one! You shall love the LORD your God with all your heart and with all your soul and with all your might. These words, which I am commanding you today, shall be on your heart. You shall teach them diligently to your sons and shall talk of them when you sit in your house and when you walk by the way and when you lie down and when you rise up. You shall bind them as a sign on your hand and they shall be as frontals on your forehead. You shall write them on the doorposts of your house and on your gates.

This passage highlights that God initiated a covenantal love relationship with Israel and provided specific instructions on how to live and thrive together as members in a faith community. The instructions were so important that the Israelites were to take great pains to teach their children and to keep the law always at the forefront with visual reminders lest they and subsequent generations forget and stumble. In the Hebrew tradition, every moment is a teaching moment about God and how to honor and love him. The book of Deuteronomy repeats previous statutes and provides additional principles to live the wise life in a manner befitting the holy, benevolent, omnipotent, and omniscient God revealed in Genesis, Exodus, Leviticus, and Numbers.

The Torah is a didactic narrative that reveals the nature and redemptive plan of the holy Creator and establishes the context for the wisdom literature in the Hebrew Bible. Proverbs 1:7 states that "the fear of the LORD is the beginning of knowledge; fools despise wisdom and instruction." Proverbs 9:10 declares that "the fear of the LORD is the beginning of wisdom and knowledge of the Holy One is understanding." Both passages use the proper name for the Lord (*Yahweh*) and take the reader back to the holy, omniscient, and omnipotent Creator and Redeemer revealed in the Torah as the context for wisdom. Fear—in the form of awe, terror, hope, reverence, and enlightenment—is a proper response when experiencing the Lord in and of the Torah, and it is the precursor and foundation for growing in wisdom, knowledge, and understanding. Fear of the Lord in a positive sense orients and focuses believers' thoughts, dispositions, and habits to align with God's character, perspectives, and priorities, in contrast to the ways of the simple and fools who lack such understanding.

The book of Proverbs is filled with insights in the form of pithy statements and maxims for making good choices in life. Most of the proverbs came from King Solomon. According to the Hebrew Bible, Solomon "spoke 3,000 proverbs and 1,005 songs" (1 Kings 4:32) and was dedicated to pondering, searching, and writing these words of truth correctly (Eccles. 12:9–14).

The book of Proverbs paints "a picture of a young man starting out in life. Two schools bid for him and both send out their literature. One is the school of wisdom and the other the school of fools."[12] The fool is portrayed as a dullard relative to the wise because of the moral stupor from despising wisdom and instruction on the good life (Prov. 1:7). The complacency of the fool eventually results in unhappiness and destruction (Prov. 1:24–32), while those who heed wisdom will live securely, at ease from the dread of evil (Prov. 1:33). Throughout the book of Proverbs, the wise pursue thoughts and habits consistent with God's priorities and understanding of how life is designed to work best, while the fool pursues fleeting, self-serving indulgences, otherwise known as folly. Both sets of people eventually reap what they sow (Prov. 6:6–11).

The word for wisdom (*chokmah*) in Proverbs is the same word used in other sections of the Hebrew Bible to describe people with different types of expertise. The term is used to convey skill at war (Isa. 10:13), as well as at technical work associated with construction and craftsmanship (Exod. 36:1–6), making of garments (Exod. 28:3), sailing and shipbuilding (Ezek. 27:8–9; Psalm 107:27), and administration (Gen. 41:33; 1 Kings 3:28; Deut. 34:9; 1 Kings 3:28; Ezek. 28:4–5). This makes the book of Proverbs a guidebook on how to become especially skilled at living.

The book of Proverbs equips people to be skilled at navigating life under relatively normal circumstances. Conversely, the book of Job reveals insights for those life experiences outside of the norm, when life goes tragically wrong, especially for "good" people like Job, a man who "who feared God and shunned evil" (Job 1:1). The book of Job is a preeminent theodicy. A *theodicy* literally means "justifying God." It is an explanation of why and how a loving and just God can allow evil in the world. The book of Job answers how and why the omniscient and omnipotent, benevolent Creator revealed in the TaNaK allows suffering and injustices, especially to those who honor him.

Job was living an upright and very blessed life when, due to no fault of his own, a series of tragedies came his way. In one day, he lost his possessions, his source of income, and his children. Soon after, he was inflicted with painful boils all over his body (Job 1 and 2). Job is joined by three friends who sit with him in silence for seven days, recognizing that words are of no comfort in the initial days of intense suffering. Later, when Job and his friends decide to speak, they engage in a series of poetic and legal-like dialogues that attempt to discern the reasons for and solutions to Job's suffering, even putting God on trial at one point, a conversation that God later judged as "words without knowledge" (Job 38:1).

Job paused during the discussions and pondered, "But where can wisdom be found? And where is the place of understanding?" (Job 28:12), given that it had been elusive in the previous conversations and appears "hidden from the eyes of all living" (Job 28:21). Job noted that "God understands its way; and He knows its place. For He looks to the ends of the earth; He sees everything under the heavens" (Job 28:23–24). Human understanding is limited to time and place, while God's knowledge and understanding has no such constraints, not only because he is omnipresent and omniscient, but also because he is the Creator and the Author of the human story (Job 28:25–27). Novelists and readers are analogies for understanding elements of wisdom described in Job 28—why it is hidden and how it is revealed. Skilled authors progressively provide clues to their characters and plots to guide their readers. The authors hide things from their readers in the initial chapters, in part to lay a foundation for understanding forthcoming truths. In this regard, revelation is progressive. Authors see the entirety of their stories, and as a result they understand why certain things happen when they do throughout the narratives, giving the authors unique wisdom at different points in the story. In contrast, the readers lack the omniscience required to be fully wise in understanding the ultimate meaning and purpose of the particulars when they emerge, as they are bound by time and place.

Authors also hide things that would take too long to explain to keep the reader engaged. In this regard, revelation is incomplete, but sufficient. Ultimate wisdom is hidden because it is too immense to be fully fathomed. God's rhetorical questions in Job 38–41 reveal that even if Job could provide the intricate answers to the barrage of questions, the answers would be too involved to be of didactic value for the immediate situation. Explaining the awe associated with witnessing sunrises and sunsets, life from the womb, soaring hawks, whales cresting, and thunderbolts would not only be time-consuming, but it risks reducing the phenomena to their irreducible parts, the equivalent of reading the notes to a grand symphony rather than enjoying the notes being played by an orchestra.

While God's ultimate wisdom is hidden, Job revealed that it can be discerned, in part, when he concluded, "And to man He [God] said 'Behold, the fear of the Lord, that is wisdom, and to turn away from evil is understanding'" (Job 28:28). Just as in Proverbs 1:7 and 9:10, the workaround to make sense out of life with partial understanding is to revere God, knowing that he alone knows things humans do not and cannot fully comprehend. The solution to ignorance of the greater mysteries of life is not necessarily more knowledge, but rather a healthy appreciation for and trust in the all-knowing and all-powerful, benevolent Creator revealed in nature (general revelation) and in the TaNaK (special revelation).

The essence of ultimate wisdom and reasons to fear God are made explicit to Job when the Lord (*Yahweh*) finally spoke (Job 38–41). God posed a plethora of rhetorical questions to Job around mysteries found in world. The implied answers serve as evidence that God created a well-coordinated and harmonious world, down to the smallest of details. The answers testify that God is a creative, just, loving, sovereign, all-knowing, and all-powerful Author of all that takes place in the universe. Going back to the metaphor of the novelists, authors craft their narratives so that the parts work together and serve larger purposes. In this regard, authors are both omnipotent and omniscient over their respective narratives. God, who created and sees the whole narrative of human existence and individual lives, alone has true wisdom since he crafted the parts to work together for some glorious, benevolent, and unfolding purpose.

The nature of wisdom when it comes to unsettling mysteries, such as suffering and injustice, is to recognize that just because divine order is obviously evident in parts of the universe does not mean it is absent in other parts. It is with this epiphany recorded in Job 42:2–5 that Job repented of his presumptions about God's character and answers God:

> I know that Thou canst do all things,
> And that no purpose of Thine can be thwarted.
> Who is this that hides counsel without knowledge?
> Therefore I have declared that which I did not understand,
> Things too wonderful for me, which I did not know.
> I have heard Thee with by the hearing of my ear:
> But now my eye sees Thee.

Ecclesiastes, like the book of Job, addresses the more existential questions of life, but from the reference point of a person who seemed to have had it all and done it all. The book of Ecclesiastes is a twelve-chapter autobiography from a person who had extreme wealth (1 Kings 10:23) and who lived life to the fullest, not in want of anything or any experience. Yet, despite a life of privilege, Solomon lamented about the ultimate futility of pleasures, possessions, prestige, and even wisdom, but he repeatedly reminded his readers that wisdom excels among all the human pursuits. While life and its various pleasures are gifts to be enjoyed, they are temporary. Solomon reflected that "here is what I have seen to be good and fitting: to eat, to drink and enjoy oneself in all one's labor in which he toils under the sun during his few years of this life which God has given him; for this is his reward" (Eccles. 5:18).

Ecclesiastes opens with its thesis statement: "Vanity of vanities, says the Preacher [Solomon], vanity of vanities! All is vanity" (1:2). The Hebrew word for vanity is habel, and it means "vapor" or "breath." Solomon used the word for "breath" to encourage his readers to automatically explore the value of life, given its relative brevity. If life is nothing more than a mere breath, a fleeting vapor, "What advantage does man have in all his work which he does under the sun?" (Eccles. 1:3).[13] Solomon unpacks the answer and reveals that life is meaningful only because it is eternal and concluded that "when all has been heard, is: fear God and keep his commandments, because this applies to every person. For God will bring every act to judgment, everything which is hidden, whether it is good or evil" (Eccles. 12:13–14). The book of James in the New Testament reiterated this truth in 4:13–15:

> Come now, you who say, "Today or tomorrow we will go to such and such a city, and spend a year there and engage in business and make a profit." Yet you do not know what your life will be like tomorrow. You are *just* a vapor that appears for a little while and then vanishes away. Instead, *you ought* to say, "If the Lord wills, we will live and also do this or that."

Additional insights into the nature of wisdom are gleaned from key passages of the prophets (Nevi'im) and writings (Ketuvi'im). At the risk of oversimplification, the essence of the Nevi'im is captured in Micah 6:8: "He has told you, O man, what is good; and what does the LORD require of you but to do justice, to love kindness, and to walk humbly with your God?" A key passage for the Ketuvi'im is Proverbs 3:5: "Trust in the LORD with all your heart and do not lean on your own understanding." Hence, wisdom is a mindset and a lifestyle that trusts and pursues God's purposes and plans.

The Old Testament wisdom literature reveals that wisdom involves nuanced perspectives and skills about life based upon a deeper understanding of how and why life works the way it does. It provides practical principles for people to be especially skilled at living during their short tenures on earth. The Old Testament reveals that wisdom is based upon a right understanding of God and His purposes, and it provides people with the context, meaning, purpose, and insight to pursue wisdom in both good and bad times.

THE NEW TESTAMENT

The New Testament is a continuation of the themes and lessons set forth in the Old Testament. Genesis 1–3 reveals that God created an ideal environment for his people to experience unhindered fellowship with him and each other in harmony with the rest of creation. Unfortunately, sin entered the world, resulting in what is called the Fall. At that point, fellowship with God and creation was broken. Ever since the Fall, God has been implementing his plan for redemption and restoration. The crucifixion and resurrection of Jesus Christ is the fulfillment of that plan.

The last book in the Bible, Revelation, reveals the fulfillment of God's plan. The symmetry and continuity of the messages in the books of the Bible between Genesis and Revelation are found in the parallels between the first three chapters and the last two chapters in Genesis and Revelation, respectively. The following chiasm illustrates the continuity of topics in Genesis and Revelation, the beginning and the end:

A Genesis 1—Heaven and earth are created

   B Genesis 2:8–15—Garden of Eden, a special place to worship God

      C Genesis 2:9, 16–17; 3:22—Trees, including a Tree of Life

      Genesis 3—The Fall

      Genesis 3:15—The first hint of Jesus Christ in his redeeming role[14]

A/ Revelation 21:1–2—The new heaven and new earth

   B/ Revelation 21:10–21—The New Jerusalem, a special place to worship God

      C/ Revelation 22:1–2—The Tree of Life

The messages between Genesis 3:15 and Revelation 21 are about restoration and establishing the Kingdom of God. While there are many other motifs in the Bible, the Kingdom of God provides a frame of reference for the other themes and storylines woven throughout the Old and New Testaments, especially in light of Jesus' words "to seek first the Kingdom of God and His righteousness" (Matt. 6:33).

Wisdom is required when we must live in two worlds with competing values and purposes: the temporal and the eternal. When the apostle Paul provided teachings for the Corinthian church on how to straddle these two kingdoms, he reported that the wisdom of the world is foolishness to God and the wisdom of God is foolishness to the world. Paul went on to state in the book of Romans that people become foolish when professing to be wise, replacing God's perspective and teachings with their own (Rom. 1:22).

The book of James, the Proverbs of the New Testament, makes a similar contrast. James provided a test for godly wisdom, in contrast to earthly wisdom, when he asked and answered the question of who is wise:

> Who among you is wise and understanding? Let him show by his good behavior his deeds in the gentleness of wisdom. But if you have bitter jealousy and selfish ambition in your heart, do not be arrogant and so lie against the truth. This wisdom is not which comes down from above, but is earthly, natural, demonic. For where jealousy and selfish ambition exists, there is disorder and every evil thing. But the wisdom from above is first pure, then peaceable, gentle, reasonable, full of mercy and good fruits, unwavering, without hypocrisy. (James 3:13–17)

James provided several concrete examples of the two types of wisdom in the remaining chapters. Temporal wisdom is evidenced by quarrels and conflicts, harsh judgments and treatment toward others; after all, the *telos* (the endgame) is about self-promotion. Divine wisdom leads to contentment and gentleness because the *telos* is about God's priorities and values.

The nature of Christian wisdom is also found in the Sermon on the Mount,[15] beginning with a list of blessings, commonly referred to as the Beatitudes, the form of which have "their roots in wisdom literature":[16]

> Blessed are the poor in spirit, for theirs is the kingdom of heaven.
> Blessed are those who mourn, for they shall be comforted.

Blessed are the gentle, for they shall inherit the earth.
Blessed are those who hunger and thirst for righteousness, for they shall be satisfied.
Blessed are the merciful, for they shall receive mercy.
Blessed are the pure in heart, for they shall see God.
Blessed are the peacemakers, for they shall be called sons of God.
Blessed are those who have been persecuted for the sake of righteousness, for theirs is the kingdom of heaven." (Matt. 5:3-10)

The blessed are those who identify with and abide by the more transcendent truths, in contrast to the alternatives implied in the eight Beatitudes listed in Matthew. The Sermon goes on to record a series of countercultural truths, such as "turn the other cheek"; "if someone forces you to go one mile, go two"; "love your enemy"; and "do not lay up for yourselves treasures upon earth." Jesus acknowledged in the message two paths, one narrow and the other wide; the former leads to life, while the latter leads to destruction (Matt. 7:13-14).

Another vivid glimpse on the nature of wisdom is found in the categories of temptation outlined in 1 John 2:15-16. The apostle John wrote: "Do not love the world, nor the things in the world. If anyone loves the world, the love of the Father is not in Him. For all that is in the world, the lust of the flesh and the lust of the eyes and the boastful pride of life, is not from the Father, but is from the world." Human temptation falls into one of the three categories: physical pleasure and comfort (the lust of the flesh), wealth and possessions (the lust of the eyes), and prestige and power (the boastful pride of life). The specific temptations with which the serpent enticed Eve in the Garden of Eden (Genesis 3:1-7) and Christ in the wilderness (Matthew 4:1-11) also fall into these same three categories. The sole pursuit of personal pleasures, possessions, and/or positions of power/prestige leads to destruction, in contrast to the quest and fruit associated with wisdom from above.

In the New Testament tradition, the wise person sought the more eternal purposes and values as his or her default framework for how to live. For Christians, wisdom begins with a right relationship with God and manifests itself in right relationships with self, others, and creation, aligning beliefs, dispositions, and behaviors with the Kingdom of God. Paul used the metaphor of ambassadors to underscore the believers' Kingdom of God status, role, and responsibilities in a temporal world that is not their home. As ambassadors, believers represent the interests of the sending kingdom in the foreign land while honoring the traditions of their hosts. Christians who are reconciled with Christ experience a new life and are given the ministry of reconciliation (2 Cor. 5:17–21). Paul went on to conclude to his fellow believers: "Therefore, we are ambassadors for Christ, as though God were entreating through us; we beg you on behalf of Christ, be reconciled to God. He made Him who knew no sin to be sin on our behalf, that we might become the righteousness of God in Him" (2 Cor. 5:20–21). The wise Christian consistently discerns how to live in this fallen world while not being of this world.

In the TaNaK and the New Testament, people are called to pursue and walk in wisdom by aligning their thoughts, dispositions, and behaviors with God's. Biblical wisdom results in being especially skilled at living, judiciously triaging temporal considerations in light of eternal truths and priorities revealed in Scripture.

THE QURAN

The Quran is considered by its adherents to be an inimitable text because it is the speech of Allah. The Quran mostly resembles the genre of prophecy, in contrast to the Bible, which contains several genres and a collection of narratives that form a complete story. The Quran contains a series of recitations given to Muhammad over a period of twenty-three years, until his death in 632 C.E., while the Bible was given to forty different authors over a period of 1,500 years. The Quran consists of 114 surahs, or chapters, ranging from three to 286 *aayah* (verses) in length. The Bible has sixty-six books of various length. The surahs are arranged from the longest to the shortest, except for the opening chapter, while the books of the Bible are grouped both chronologically and thematically.

There are two broad and different sets of revelation in the Quran not readily evident in its current structure of the chapters arranged from the longest to the shortest. Ninety-two of the surahs were revelations that occurred during Muhammad's last thirteen years in Mecca, and the remaining twenty-two surahs were from his final ten years in Medina. The message in the Quran takes on a different tenor, and, some would say, message, because of the different Muslim experiences in Mecca and Medina.[17] The two divisions have distinct contrasts, with the former emphasizing more tolerance, faith, prophecy, and union with Allah, and the latter focusing on judgment, deeds, fulfillment of prophecy, and treatment of others.[18]

The mingling of the revelations from the two different time periods and the inimitable nature of the Quran presents hermeneutical[19] challenges to discern the nature of wisdom in the Quran. While the Quran references wisdom (*hikmah*), it is not as nuanced or explicit as the references to wisdom given in the Old and New Testaments. While the duties associated with the five pillars of Islam are clear,[20] the Quran does not provide specific guidelines for navigating life's dilemmas when submitting to Allah. Mir Tamin Ansary, in his *Destiny Disrupted: A History of the World Through Islamic Eyes*, wrote:

> The Quran did not explicitly address many questions that cropped up in real life. As a matter of fact, most of the Holy Book spoke in very general terms: Stop sinning; behave yourself; have a heart; you *will* be judged; hell is an awful place; heaven is wonderful; be grateful for all that God has given you: trust in God; obey God; yield to God—such is the gist of the message one gets from much of the Holy Book. Even where the Quran gets specific, it is often open to interpretation.[21]

The limited explicit attention to the elements of wisdom can be in part explained in that the Quran explicitly recognizes the truth of the Bible, albeit with some provisions and self-reported corrections (2:4, 2:136, 3:3, 3:48, 4:163–171, 5:46, 5:110, 10:108–109, 17:2, 61:5–6, and 87:16–19).[22] Surah 5:46 states that the truth of previous revelation is provided as a source of guidance for the dutiful: "And We sent after them in their footsteps Jesus, son of Mary, verifying that which was before him of the Torah; and We gave him the Gospel containing guidance and light, and verifying that which was before it of the Torah, and a guidance and an admonition for the dutiful."[23] Surah 5:68 reiterates that the path of good is realized by obedience to the truths found in previous scriptures: "Say: O People of the Book, you follow no good till you observe the Torah and the Gospel and that which is revealed to you from the Lord." Surah 6:91 states that "the Book of Moses brought a light and guidance to men." Surah 29:46 states that Muslims "believe in that which has been revealed to us [Muslims] and revealed to you [People of the Book], and our God and your God is One, and to Him we submit."

In addition to acknowledging the wisdom of the Jewish and Christian holy texts, the Quran claims that it is provided to "be a guidance to men" (2:185) and whose "verses are characterized by wisdom" (Surah 11:1). The opening surah to the Quran beseeched Allah to guide believers on the right path (1:5). A few verses later, in surah 2:2, the Quran reads, "This Book, there is no doubt in it, is a guide to those who keep their duty." The Quran also refers to itself as the Book of Wisdom (2:129, 2:151, 2:231, 4:113, 31:3). Surah 26:2 states that "these are the verses of the Book that makes manifested" and is interpreted to mean that "the Holy Quran makes manifest all that is needed for a right development of the human faculties, and it also makes manifest the whole truth." Surah 24:1 states that the Quran is provided so that followers "can be mindful" to attend to the truth in their words and actions, and surah 38:29 invites readers "to ponder over its verses" so that they "may mind," or rightly attend to, right thoughts and practices.

One of the defining elements of the Islamic faith is submission to Allah,[24] a command repeated throughout the Quran and cogently captured in surah 4:25: "And who is better in religion than he who submits himself entirely to Allah while doing good and follows the faith of Abraham, the upright one?" The call to submission to Allah provides a telling clue to the nature of wisdom in the Quran. Like in the Bible, where the fear of the Lord is the beginning of wisdom, submission to Allah is the beginning of wisdom in the Quran.

Surah 25:67 provides another insight to the need and nature of wisdom that is reminiscent of Aristotle's Golden Mean: "And they who, when they spend, are neither extravagant nor parsimonious, and the just mean is ever between these." The need for a just mean is the temptation to go to the extreme when multiple options exist, in this case, handling resources. Another example of specific wisdom advice is found in surah 52:20 and is reminiscent of Solomon's words in Ecclesiastes: "Know that this world's life is only sport and play and gaiety and boasting among yourselves and a vying in the multiplication of wealth and children. . . . And this world's life is naught but a source of vanity." Surah 42:38, similar to Proverbs 11:14 and 15:2, lauds the use of counselors for success, recognizing that individuals have limited perspectives. The Quran highlights competing perspectives and requires the faithful to discern the appropriate balance and path.

The opening surah (*Fatihah*) of the Quran provides the most compelling insight to the nature of wisdom to be found in the text. The *Fatihah*, also referenced in surah 15:87 as the "seven oft-repeated verses," are to be recited with every Muslim prayer. In his translation of the Quran, Abdullah Yusuf Ali stated that "every Muslim repeats these seven verses at least thirty-times a day, no other portion of the Holy Quran being repeated so often."[25] The *Fatihah*, like all the other surahs, except for surah 9, have the heading *Bismillah alRahman alrahim—In the name of Allah, the Beneficent, the Merciful*. The *Bismillah* serves a critical element in each surah that it appears. Surah 1 reads:

In the name of Allah, the Beneficent, the Merciful.

1. Praise to Allah, the Lord of the worlds,
2. The Beneficent, the Merciful,
3. Master of the day of Requital.
4. Thee do we serve and Thee do we beseech for help.
5. Guide us on the right path,
6. The path of those upon whom Thou hast bestowed favors,
7. Not those upon whom wrath is brought down, nor those who go astray.

Ali noted the "*Bismillah* is the quintessence of the chapter *Fatihah*, in the same manner as the latter is the quintessence of the Quran itself."[26] Reciting the *Bismillah* orients the Muslim to internalize an attitude of a humble and gracious servant to an all-merciful and forever-merciful Allah and by such acknowledgment consciously abstain from actions that would displease Allah. The *Bismillah* reveals that the continual mindfulness of Allah and his merciful beneficence is the beginning of wisdom.

The first three verses in surah 1 reveal the nature of Allah, the all-and ever-beneficent and merciful Allah of all who rightly judges and recompenses all friendly and unfriendly acts. Recognizing a time of judgment is another source of wisdom, acknowledging that some paths are better than others. The wise seek the help from the beneficent and merciful Allah to stay on the right path (1:5), in contrast to the wrong path, which leads people astray (1:7).

In the Quran, wisdom is found in submission to Allah. The consistent reciting of the Quran puts the Muslim in touch with the actual words of Allah and imposes a dialectical and existential angst that the faithful would imbibe the divine to discern and stay on the right path.

Less space in this primer is devoted to the nature of wisdom from the Quran than from the Bible for several reasons. First, the Quran is much shorter, slightly one-tenth of the words found in the Bible. Second, the Quran is more a collection of sayings and admonishments to submit to Allah in contrast to the didactic narratives found in the Bible. Third, the Quran is arranged from longest to shortest surahs, in contrast to themes and lessons.[27] Fourth, the Quran, as the reported actual words/language of Allah, is intended to be recited in Arabic for its full import to be realized, where the Bible is meant to be studied to discern the inspired authors' intended meaning.

While all sacred texts have exegetical challenges, the structure and content of the Quran present additional difficulties to discover the text's meaning. Islamic scholar Tarif Khalidi noted in his introduction to his English translation of the Quran that "the very allusiveness of the text, its impersonality, its meta-historical tone, seem almost deliberately to de-emphasize context."[28] Despite the lack of a cohesive structure and exegetical challenges, there are enough clues to discern the nature of wisdom from the Quran.

The Quran, as with the previous Scriptures of the Old and New Testaments, reveals that humans are spiritual beings who, while eternal, temporarily dwell as physical beings in a fallen world. Their tenure on earth presents many options and temptations for people to pursue. These three faith traditions emphasize that an all-loving, merciful, and wise Creator provides a path for eternal life and guidance for life on earth. The Judeo-Christian text emphasizes loving obedience to God in the context of a redeemed and unconditional relationship with God, while the Quran focuses on unyielding submission in the context of conditional favor with Allah. In the Quran, submission to Allah is the path to wisdom, a message underscored by the fact that *Islam* literally means "submission." This submission allows Muslims to make life choices consistent with Allah's path for his created beings.

THE SACRED TEXTS IN HINDUISM

Hinduism is the more mystical and eclectic of the four faith traditions cited in this primer, due in part to its syncretic history. Hinduism emerged from the numerous small tribes living along and beyond the Indus River as early as 1600 B.C.E. These tribes developed social and political connections and synthesized their beliefs and spiritual practices over time. As a result, Hinduism is technically not a single religion as it recognizes several deities and correspondingly embraces many diverse traditions with an emphasis on personal spirituality. Hinduism, unlike Judaism, Christianity, and Islam, is polytheistic and lacks a historical founder and ecclesiastic authority.[29]

The corpus of Hindu writings is vast and varied, in contrast to the Bible and the Quran, which consist of corresponding sets of texts in self-contained books. The extensive and lengthy set of Hindu literature falls into one of two general categories. The two general categories of Hindu sacred texts and corresponding writings are listed in Figure 2.1. The Sruti consists of the primary and earliest set of Hindu texts known as the Vedas. They contain

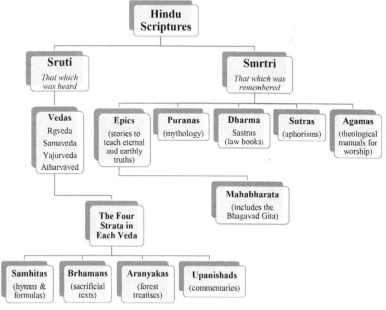

Figure 2.1. Sacred Texts of Hinduism

insights and teachings revealed to the *rishis* (the mythical founders of Hinduism who, through meditation, received the messages of the Vedas). The Vedas are the more sacred of all of the Hindu religious literature. *Veda* is from the Sanskrit root *vid*, which means "to know." The implication is that the Vedas contain important knowledge to the nature of reality necessary to find harmony with the universe. There are four Vedas: Rgveda, Samaveda, Yajurveda, and the Atharvaveda.[30]

For many Hindus, the Vedas are the "most authoritative and sacred" of the Hindu texts.[31] The Vedas are the chief foundational texts for the subsequent Hindu scriptures and are reportedly the source of divine knowledge and wisdom. The four Vedas primarily consist of hymns intended to inform and guide Hindu practices and customs and correct behavior. The Vedas have four sections. The primary, or the Vedas proper, known as the Samhitas, consists of mantras that personify the forces of nature that ancient Hindus incanted. The second element, the Brahmanas, involves ritual and liturgy and consists of primarily manuals for the priests. The Aranyakas, the forest books, is the third section of the Vedas and provides mystical insights gained from observing nature itself. These were originally guidebooks for the hermit and emerging sage. The Upanishads are philosophical musings and commentaries and extend the messages found in the earlier portions of the Vedas.[32]

The Upanishads mark the transition to classical Hinduism, from the sacrificial cultic practices of ancient Hinduism. The etymology of *Upanishad* is "to come near (*upa*) to sit (*ni-shad*)," so as to glean profound and important insights from a teacher. The invitation is for the serious student to come and learn what is of ultimate importance.[33]

The Smriti is the second and largest category of Hindu literature. While the Sruti are the revealed sacred knowledge (i.e., the Vedas), the Smriti are the sacred traditions, or "what is remembered by human teachers, in contradistinction to what is directly heard or revealed to the sages."[34] The Puranas informs much of contemporary Hinduism and consists of eighteen major and eighteen minor books on the mythology related to the Hindu deities, specifically Brahma, Vishnu, and Shiva. The Agamas are numerous writings related to the various deities in the Hindu belief system. The Epics are long devotional poems, of which the Bhagavad Gita is by far the more important in popular and contemporary Hindu thought. Other writings include the Sastra class of texts.[35]

The size and polytheistic nature of the Hindu sacred corpus does not lend itself to a cohesive and singular narrative as found in the Bible and the Quran. Given the syncretic features, scope, and length of the whole corpus of Hindu scripture, this primer limited its observations on the nature of Hindu wisdom taught in the Upanishads and the Bhagavad Gita. While the other Hindu texts are informative, limited space in this primer cannot do justice to their size and scope, especially since it is somewhat redundant, as the other texts build off the extensive Vedas and distillation of that teaching explicated in the Upanishads.

Upanishadic scholar Robert Hume noted that the "Upanishads are the first recorded attempts of the Hindus at systematic philosophizing."[36] He observed that the Upanishads lack a formal structure and continuity of message within and among the various Upanishads and do not lend themselves to a systematic teaching found in the prophetic religions. Hume stated:

> [The Upanishads] represent the earnest efforts of the profound thinkers of early India to resolve the problems of the origin, the nature, and the destiny of man and of the universe, or—more technically—the meaning and value of "knowing" and "being." Though they contain some fanciful ideas, naïve speculations, and inadequate conclusions, yet they are replete with sublime conceptions and with intuitions of universal truth.[37]

He concluded that it is "clear that the Upanishads are not homogenous products, cogently presenting a philosophic theory, but that they are compilations from different sources recording the 'guesses at truth' of the early Indians. A single, well-articulated system cannot be deduced from them."[38]

While the Upanishads corpus lacks an explicit cohesive structure and consistent message, wisdom is found in the universal and transcendent themes realized when the Upanishads are studied as a whole. For example:

> In the Upanishads are set forth, in concrete example as well as in dogmatic instruction, two opposing theories of life: an ignorant, narrow, selfish way of life which seeks temporary, unsatisfying, unreal ends; and a way of life which seeks to relate itself to the Supreme Reality of the universe, so as to escape from the needless misery of ordinary existence into undying bliss.[39]

CHAPTER 2

The most frequently recurring phrase in the Upanishads, *ya evain veda* "(he who knows this)" alludes to its essential message and teaching, to know "the Real of the real" (Brihad 2.1.20).[40] The first realization is that the many earlier Vedic and Brahmanic gods were a clue that Brahma is "all the gods" (Brihad 1.4.6), for "verily, this whole world is Brahma" (Maitri 4.6). It is this realization that inspires one to attain unity with Brahma, which will lead to liberation—"He who knows Brahma as the real, as knowledge, as the infinite . . . obtains all desires" (Taittiriya 2.1). True knowledge is mystical unity with Brahma, for "He, verily, who knows that supreme Brahma, becomes very Brahma" (Mundaka 3.2.9), for by knowing God one is "released from all fetters" (Svetasvatara 1.8; 2.15; 4.16; 5.14; 6.13).

The Upanishads distinguish two soul states. The *Atman* (Soul), which is united with Brahma, and the *atman* (soul), "who, being overcome by the bright or the dark fruits of action enters a good or an evil womb, so that his course is downward or upward" (Maitri 3.1). Because of ignorance, the true unity between the *Atman*/Brahma is not readily and easily realized or experientially known. Until true knowledge is achieved, the *atman* (soul with a small *s*, or atman with a small *a*) has a choice between two paths. One path leads to the gods and the other to the fathers (Brihad 6.2.2; Chandogya 5.3.2). The paths are a continuous cycle of birth and death that is determined by one's previous deeds (*karma*), with final liberation (*moksha*) realized when one achieves unity with Brahma (Katha 3.7.8.9; Mundaka 2.2.8; Maitri 1.4). The following prayer provided at the time of sacrifice captures the Hindu's ultimate quest while on the path to be released from all earthly fetters to experience oneness with Brahma: "From the unreal lead me to the real, from darkness lead me to the light, from death lead me to immortality" (Brihad 1.3.28).

The Upanishads teach that desires are the root of all actions and reveal the path one is traveling. When one desires exclusively the Soul (*Atman*), one can love purely. The Brihad describes how love for Soul makes everything dear (Brihad 4.5.6; 4.4.7; 5.10) and that desires for more temporal and self-serving pursuits mark the other path. Unfortunately, the individual soul has dark, passionate, and miserable qualities that provide false illusions of reality that interfere with achieving transcendent oneness with Brahma. Maitri 6.30 describes that people full of desire are distracted and go "into a state of self-conceit" and that "the pathway to Brahma in this world" is freedom from desire. The specifics of the baser qualities are not explicated in detail in the Upanishads but are inferred by the Upanishads' emphasis on paradoxical teaching that the way to peace is the desire to have no desires. The Bhagavad Gita[41] reiterates the theme to abandon earthly desires when stating, "When he renounces all desires and acts without cravings, possessiveness, or individuality, he finds peace" (2.71).

As actions are the manifestations of desires, the Upanishads take on the role of introducing the early teachings on the importance and consequence of one's action, known as *karma*.[42] Given the eternal nature of one's soul taught in Hinduism, what happens to the soul until unity with Brahma is achieved? The cycle of rebirth and death allows souls to keep trying until they get it right. The teaching of *karma* acknowledges that the quality of one's attempt in the current life is rewarded proportionately in subsequent attempts.

According as one acts, according as one conducts himself, so does he become. The doer of good becomes good. The doer of evil becomes evil. One becomes virtuous by virtuous action, bad by bad action. But people say: "A person is made of desires only." As is his desire, such is his resolve; as is his resolve, such the action he performs; what action he performs, that he procures for himself. (Brihad 4.5.9)

The Kaushitaki 1.2 states that "either as a worm, or as moth, or as a fish, or as a bird, or as a snake, or as a tiger, or as a person, or as some other in this or that condition, he is born again here according to his deeds, according to his knowledge." People's *karma* determines their respective fate in their present and subsequent lives. The message in *karma* is that some actions are better than others and that the wise are able to discern and act accordingly.

The Upanishads provide several teachings and practices that generate good *karma* and final liberation (*moksha*). Prasna 1.10 notes that "they who seek *Atman* by austerity, chastity, faith, and knowledge . . . they do not return." Maitri 4.4 indicates that Brahma is apprehended through knowledge, austerity, and Hindu meditation.[43] Katha 6.11 highlights the power of yoga[44]—"The firm holding back of the senses. Then one becomes undistracted. Yoga, truly, is the origin and the end." Katha 2.12 underscores that "by considering him as God, through the Yoga-study of what pertains to self, the wise man leaves joy and sorrow behind." Svetavatara 1.3 reports that "those who are practiced in mediation and yoga have beheld the self-power of God hidden by his attributes. He, the One, rules overall these causes, all those from time to self."

To live rightly is to be on the path that leads to enlightened knowledge. The nature of wisdom in the Hindu text is insight and enlightenment about Atman/Brahma such that one becomes free of all desires. It is through Hindu meditation, the abandonment of desire and want (i.e., austerity), the spiritual exercise of focusing the mind and body (i.e., ancient yoga), the study of the knowledge (i.e., the Vedas), and virtuous actions (*karma*) that one can achieve ultimate liberation (*moksha*). While the Upanishads teach the path to wisdom, they also highlight the fact that gurus are necessary to achieve the highest levels of enlightenment. In Sanskrit, *guru* literally means "dispeller of darkness."[45]

The Bhagavad Gita ("The Song of God") is a portion of the Mahabharata epic that, like the Upanishads, is a distillation of Hindu teachings.[46] While technically part of the Smriti, many consider it part of the Sruti since it records a conversation between Lord Krishna[47] and the warrior prince, Arjuna, making it a form of direct revelation. Arjuna is conflicted about going to war, and Lord Krishna instructs Arjuna on duty (*dharma*) and guides Arjuna to the next level of wisdom required to justify war. Lord Krishna also uses the opportunity to provide Arjuna with additional wisdom for everyday life and principles for achieving *moksha* (final liberation).

Early in his angst about going into battle, Arjuna asked Lord Krishna, "What is the mark of a man of steady wisdom, the man immersed in enstasy?[48] How does one speak—this man of steadied thought? How sit? How walk?" (Gita, 2.54). Lord Krishna answered, "When a man puts from him all desires that prey upon the mind, Himself (*atamana*) contented in the self alone, then is he called a man of steady wisdom" (Gita, 2.55). Concepts of duty (*dharma*), action (*karma*), focus (*yoga*), meditation, sacrifice, austerity, study of "scripture," and renunciation of desires referenced in the Upanishads receive additional attention throughout the Gita as to how "wisdom is kindled" (Gita, 4.27).

In Gita 16, 23, and 24, Lord Krishna underscores with Arjuna the didactic value of Hindu scripture as a source of wisdom and liberation:

Whoso forsakes the ordinance of Scripture
And lives at the whim of his own desires,

Wins not perfection, [finds] not comfort,
[Treads not] the highest Way.
Therefore, let Scripture be the norm,
Determining right and wrong.
Once thou dost know what the ordinance of Scripture bids thee do,
Then shouldst thou here perform the works [therein prescribed].

The Gita teaches that practical wisdom is the path of balance in life to achieve enlightened wisdom associated with mystical oneness with Lord Krishna. According to the Gita, "An individual's level of wisdom could be nil or negative (indulgence in 'devil or dark ways'), low (indulgence in 'passion or selfish and foolish ways'), moderate ('goodness,' or the highest possible (with status of 'yogi'). Yogis are rare: 'Among thousands of men but one, maybe, will strive for self-perfection.'"[49]

The Gita, like the Upanishads, make explicit that life is ultimately a battle within oneself, and with others and society. People inherit respective responsibilities and duties (*dharma*). Their actions generate corresponding *karma* and their subsequent fate in the cycle of birth and rebirth (*samsara*). Those who perform wisely eventually experience liberation (*moksha*).

The primary message of the Vedas, and the core theology of Hinduism, is for adherents to experience enlightenment, complete oneness with the divine. Real knowledge is attained through Hindu meditation, the study of knowledge, austerity, ancient yoga, and duty. Hindu enlightenment results in transcendence, so the person may live wisely in relation to the temporal, detached enough from worldly pursuits, free from distractions, to become attuned with the divine.

CONCLUSION

The Hebrew Bible, the New Testament, the Quran, and the sacred texts of Hinduism attest to the same human dilemma, albeit with sometimes contradictory explanations and answers. People are eternal beings temporarily residing in a physical world where something went amiss. Each text provides its own transcendent narrative of what is true and of ultimate meaning, which both informs and guides their respective believers on how to be the most skilled at living in a broken and fallen world.

The overview of wisdom from the sacred texts reveals that the structure of wisdom involves two major storylines: the temporal and the eternal, the latter of which governs the former. Implied in navigating temporal scenarios with eternal priorities are multiple earthly and eternal storylines at any one point in time. For example, when it comes to money, the Bible provides three different sets of instructions. The wise leave an inheritance for their children's children (Prov. 13:22), give generously to the poor (Deut. 15:11), and provide for their immediate family (1 Tim. 5:8). How much should people save for their grandchildren, give to charity, and spend now to help family members do well? The transcendent storyline is that money is a stewardship issue with competing temporal spending options, in contrast to the solely temporal view, which can lead to the love of money and corresponding evils (1 Tim. 6:10).

Wisdom in the theological traditions is a nuanced understanding of life based upon earth- and heaven-bound perspectives. It begins with a right knowledge and understanding of God (e.g., "the fear of the LORD is the beginning of wisdom" [Psalm 9:10], and the *Bismillah* in the Quran). Wisdom is a metanarrative that makes sense of life on both sides of the grave for people to live a "good" earthly life based upon revealed truths and eternal priorities.

REFLECTION AND DISCUSSION QUESTIONS

1. How and why do theologians consider theology to be the queen of the sciences and philosophy to be its servant?
2. What is the relationship between general and special revelation in the theological tradition, and how and why is the distinction necessary and useful for understanding the nature of truth and wisdom?
3. What is the relationship between wisdom literature in the Bible, the other books of the Bible, and the corresponding lesson on the nature of wisdom?
4. What does it mean to be especially skilled at living, and how does one become skilled at living according to Proverbs?

5. How and why is submission to Allah a defining element in the Islamic tradition, and what is the corresponding lesson on the nature of wisdom?

6. What is the *Bismillah* in the Quran, and what does it suggest about the source and nature of wisdom?

7. What are the relationships between enlightenment, desire, duty, liberation, and wisdom as outlined in the Upanishads and the Gita?

8. How do the theological perspectives on the nature of wisdom support and/or enhance the philosophical understandings of the nature of wisdom presented in Chapter 1?

3

EMPIRICAL
PERSPECTIVES ON
WISDOM

Charles Darwin used systematic observations, measurements, and analysis to make inferences on the nature of reality in his *On the Origin of Species*, published in 1859. His treatment on natural selection demonstrated that one did not necessarily need philosophy or theology to explain the laws of nature, and it established the utility of the scientific or empirical method. With its roots in the Scientific Revolution (1543–1687), the empirical method of testing hypotheses and verifying conclusions through systematic experimentation provided ways to improve society and became the foundation for the Enlightenment (1651–1794), the Industrial Revolution (1769–1914), and contemporary science and technology. The scientific method was revolutionary when it emerged, as it led to new discoveries and ways of knowing that supported and contradicted previously held philosophical and theological explanations about the nature of reality. Empiricism gave way to naturalism, a worldview that "stands opposed to supernaturalism [theism], insisting that the 'the world of nature should form a single sphere without incursions from outside by souls or spirits, divine or human.'"[1]

While the empirical model yielded great benefits to society and systemized knowledge on the nature of reality, it restricted research to only that which was observable and measurable. As a result, concepts such as the soul, spirituality, or wisdom received less attention. Scholars and researchers in the social sciences have only recently endeavored to use the empirical tradition to develop models to capture the essence of wisdom with the goal of helping people develop and practice wisdom.

Researchers have utilized implicit and explicit approaches to operationalize wisdom. The former synthesizes people's folk conceptions of wisdom while the latter uses psychological and sociological constructs to operationally define wisdom. Complexity science, while not specifically in the domain of wisdom research, captures the underlying architecture common to all dynamic systems and provides a metatheory on wisdom in the empirical tradition. What follows is a brief review of the seminal research on wisdom, an explanation of the bridge between complexity science and wisdom research, and a synthesis of the findings.

IMPLICIT AND EXPLICIT THEORIES OF WISDOM

Implicit theories of wisdom are based upon people's cultural and personal concepts of wisdom, the common perceptions of who is wise, and the study of aphorisms and proverbs. Each culture esteems certain virtues and values over others, making what might be wise in one culture appear foolish in another. For example, acquiescing to authority out of respect may be prudent in one culture while asserting autonomy by speaking truth to power may be respected in another. The primary empirical method for developing implicit theories of wisdom is to interview cohorts and identify themes and patterns from the respective narratives. Implicit theories of wisdom are based upon perspectives and actions relative to specific reference groups.

In contrast, explicit approaches to the study of wisdom take constructs from psychology and sociology and attempt to quantify and qualify the various attributes, causes, and consequences of wisdom. The primary empirical method for developing explicit theories of wisdom is to measure the various definitions and facets of wisdom based upon previous theories and establish correlations. For example, if the ability to deal with ambiguity is a facet of wisdom, to what degree is it present with other identified aspects of wisdom?

Erik Erikson (1902–1994), one of the first developmental psychologists, used implicit and explicit approaches to understand wisdom.

Erikson posited that wisdom is the result of a successfully navigated life, and he identified eight stages of psychosocial development, listed in Table 3.1.[2] Erikson's schedule of virtues and psychosocial crises emerged after years of listening to life histories from a psychoanalytical framework and from his study of students at Harvard and Yale universities, World War II veterans, civil rights workers, and Sioux and Yurok Native Americans. Each stage, when successfully navigated, yields a strength and a schedule of virtues. As indicated in Table 3.1, wisdom is the eighth and optimal virtue.

Table 3.1. Stages of Psychosocial Development

Stage	Psychosocial Crises	Human Strength/Virtue
Infancy	Basic Trust vs. Basic Mistrust	Hope
Early Childhood	Autonomy vs. Shame and Doubt	Will
Play Age	Initiative vs. Guilt	Purpose
School Age	Industry vs. Inferiority	Competence
Adolescence	Identity vs. Identity Confusion	Fidelity
Young Adulthood	Intimacy vs. Isolation	Love
Adulthood	Generativity vs. Stagnation	Care
Old Age	Integrity vs. Despair	Wisdom

In an earlier work, Erikson defined *wisdom* as a "detached concern for life itself, in the face of death itself."[3] According to Erikson, one can practice transcendence beyond death by looking backward to put life in perspective (in contrast to the theological tradition of looking to the present for redemption and forward to give life meaning).

Implicit theories of wisdom attempt to identify what sets wise people apart. Psychologists and scholars Vivian Clayton and Jim Birren were pioneers in the fields of gerontology and wisdom. In their seminal study on wisdom, they had participants from different age groups describe a wise person, and they identified eleven dimensions of wisdom: Experience, Intuition, Introspection, Pragmatism, Understanding, Gentleness, Empathy, Intelligence, Peacefulness, Knowledge, and Humor.[4] Holliday and Chandler, in their book, *Wisdom: Explorations in Adult Competence*, took a similar approach and identified five factors that describe the wise person: Exceptional Understanding, Sound Judgment and Communication Skills, General Competence, Proper Interpersonal Skills, and Social Unobtrusiveness.[5]

While both lists overlap, they also have differences, suggesting that there might be some universal features to the nature of wisdom, but also that it is contextual.

Robert Sternberg, an eminent cognitive psychologist and prolific scholar on intelligence, creativity, and wisdom, asked professors of art, business, philosophy, and physics to describe the characteristics of ideally intelligent, creative, and wise persons in their respective fields of study, and he obtained over one hundred behaviors from each population. He then had a corresponding sample of people rank the descriptors in their respective fields of study. Using a multidimensional scaling and correlational analyses, Sternberg identified six dimensions with corresponding behaviors to develop his implicit theory of wisdom.

1. Reasoning ability: Ten behaviors related to the unique ability to make important connections and distinctions and solve problems.
2. Sagacity: Ten behaviors related to the ability to be thoughtful and caring.
3. Learning from ideas and environment: Three behaviors related to ideation and perceptiveness.
4. Judgment: Seven behaviors related to being a clear thinker prior to speaking.
5. Expeditious use of information: Eight behaviors related to reflective learning from experiences and flexibility of mind.
6. Perspicacity: Four behaviors related to discernment on the side of right and truth. [6]

Sternberg noted two personality characteristics of the wise person in contrast to the intelligent and creative individual. The wise person is comfortable dealing with ambiguity, given that much of life is dealing with "unending dialectic with each other and with the world, with the result that truly unambiguous situations never exist."[7] In contrast, the intelligent person wants to "solve" ambiguity, while the creative person will tolerate ambiguity and vacillate between various perspectives. The second attribute of the wise person is his or her approach to handling obstacles. According to Sternberg, "the wise person seeks to understand obstacles—why they are there, what they mean, how general or specific they are, and what their implications are for others as well as oneself."[8] In contrast, the intelligent person solves problems as they are framed in the moment, and the creative person reframes the problem to develop novel outcomes.

Sociologist and professor Monika Ardelt synthesized the works of Clayton and Birren, Holliday and Chandler, and Sternberg and concluded that they have in common cognitive, reflective, and affective wisdom descriptors.[9] She noted that while a standard definition for wisdom has yet to emerge, there "is a consensus that wisdom is a multifaceted and multidimensional concept and that the multiple facets and dimensions reinforce each other."[10] Ardelt constructed a three-dimensional wisdom scale (3D-WS) based on her own interviews with older adults and conducted various validity and reliability studies, concluding that the instrument was reliable and valid in assessing the latent variable of wisdom. The three dimensions are:

Cognitive

The cognitive dimension of wisdom refers to a person's ability to understand life, that is, to comprehend the significance and deeper meaning of phenomena and events, particularly with regard to intrapersonal and interpersonal matters (Ardelt 2000b; Blanchard-Fields and Norris 1995; Chandler and Holliday 1990; Kekes 1983; Sternberg 1990a). This includes knowledge of the positive and negative aspects of human nature, of the inherent limits of knowledge, and of life's unpredictability and uncertainties. Items that belong to the cognitive component of wisdom should assess people's ability and willingness to understand a situation or phenomenon thoroughly, as well as people's knowledge of the ambiguity of human nature and of life in general.[11]

Reflective

The reflective dimension is a prerequisite for the development of the cognitive dimension of wisdom. A deeper understanding of life is only possible if one can perceive reality as it is without any major distortions. To do this, one needs to engage in reflective thinking by looking at phenomena and events from many different perspectives to develop self-awareness and self-insight. This practice will gradually reduce one's self-centeredness, subjectivity, and projections, and increase one's insight into the true nature of things, including the motivations of one's own and other people's behavior (Chandler and

Holliday 1990; Clayton 1982; Csikszentmihalyi and Rathunde 1990; Kramer 1990; Orwoll and Achenbaum 1993; Rathunde 1995; Taranto 1989).[12]

Ardelt provided additional observations on the reflective dimension:

> The reflective dimension of wisdom is the crucial component among the three because it encourages the development of both the cognitive and the affective elements of wisdom (Ardelt 2000a). A deeper understanding of life and human nature arises after the consideration of multiple points of view and an overcoming of subjectivity and projections. Similarly, projections do not only distort the perception of reality, but they are often accompanied by negative emotions and feelings such as depression, anger, or even hatred. However, through the practice of (self-) reflection, people on the path to wisdom learn not to react to unpleasant sensations, to accept the reality of the present moment, and to acknowledge and understand their own and other persons' motives and behavior (Hart 1987). Hence, genuine feelings of sympathy and compassion for others will emerge only after a decrease in self-centeredness through the transcendence of subjectivity and projections (Clayton and Birren 1980; Kramer 1990; Pascual- Leone 1990).[13]

Affective

A diminished self-centeredness and a better understanding of people's behavior, in turn, are likely to improve one's affective emotions and demeanor toward others and tend to increase sympathetic and compassionate love (Csikszentmihalyi and Rathunde 1990; Levitt 1999; Pascual-Leone 1990). Items for the affective dimension of wisdom should, therefore, assess the presence of positive emotions and behavior toward other beings, such as feelings and acts of sympathy and compassion, and the absence of indifferent or negative emotions and behavior toward others.[14]

Ardelt concluded that wisdom is "a personality characteristic rather than a performance-based characteristic" that is "compatible to Erikson's (1982) stage mode of human development that describes wisdom as a virtue."[15] Regardless, if one is wise or if one demonstrates wise behavior at times, implicit theories of wisdom seem to be in agreement that wisdom contains cognitive, reflective, and affective elements—features that would also emerge in the explicit theories on wisdom.

The explicit theories of wisdom attempt to capture how wise thinking is different from knowing, understanding, and creativity. A leading explicit approach to the study on wisdom originated from the work of Paul Baltes and his colleagues at the Max Planck Institute for Human Development in Berlin, Germany. Their pioneering work is established in the literature as the Berlin Wisdom Research Project or the Berlin Wisdom Paradigm. The Institute was founded in 1961 to provide scientific insights on human flourishing and education for the betterment of society. Baltes served as the director of the Center for Lifespan Psychology at the Max Planck Institute for Human Development from 1980 to 2004. During his tenure, he launched into the scientific exploration of wisdom.

The research on wisdom by Baltes and his colleagues emerged from their studies on successful aging. They reported that "the concept of wisdom became the rallying point" for their "subsequent search for the hidden treasure of old age."[16] They noted in the chronicle of their wisdom research that "meanwhile, our work on wisdom is not only informed by the positive aspects of human aging. On the contrary, we presently conceptualized wisdom as an instantiation of a construct that for all phases and contexts of life, offers the potential for defining the means and ends toward a good or even optimal life."[17]

Once identifying wisdom as the optimal virtue for healthy functioning (like Erikson), Baltes and his colleagues combined philosophical and psychological constructs related to wisdom and developed both implicit and explicit theories of wisdom. The Berlin Wisdom Paradigm developed wisdom-related performance measures (WRP) and conceptualized "wisdom as an expertise in the meaning and conduct of life" or what they refer to as the "fundamental pragmatics of life."[18] According to Ursula Staudinger, a colleague of Baltes, the "fundamental pragmatics of life refer to deep insight and sound judgment about the essence of the human condition and the ways and means of planning, managing, and understanding a good life. The term 'expertise' implies that wisdom is a highly differentiated body of insights and skills usually acquired through experience and practice."[19]

Baltes and his colleagues presented difficult life problems to participants in their studies and evaluated their responses against five qualitative criteria. The five criteria were based upon research on expertise, lifespan development, cognitive development, and cultural-historical analyses of wisdom. The criteria were:

1. Rich factual knowledge on the fundamental pragmatics of life: Knowledge of human nature and development, interpersonal relations, and social norms.
2. Rich procedural knowledge on the fundamental pragmatics of life: Navigating life goals and managing conflict.
3. Lifespan contextualism: Reciprocal and dynamic relationships among family, education, work, and friends.
4. Value relativism and tolerance: Balance between and comfort with competing individual and collective interests and values with focus on virtuous outcomes and life priorities.
5. Recognition and management of uncertainty: Acknowledging and managing limitations on knowing and ability to predict and control the future.[20]

They compared the performance of professionals (e.g., clinical psychologists) whose work required judgments on par with those outlined in the five criteria with other professionals whose occupations followed more scripted judgments (e.g., architecture, journalism, business administration, medical technology). They then compared the findings with twenty-one wisdom nominees and found that they excelled in the various criteria previously identified. As the work on wisdom progressed, Baltes and his colleagues discovered that the "wiser" people developed mental scripts around the identified criteria. They concluded that "bodies of wisdom-related knowledge are available but generally not bound together until mental representations or mental scripts such as the wisdom concept are used as a coordinating cue."[21] Accordingly, "wisdom can be viewed as a metaheuristic that activates and organizes knowledge about the fundamental pragmatics of life in the service of optimizing an integration between mind and virtue."[22] As a metaheuristic, wisdom guides what and how to attend to multiple and competing demands at any particular juncture and discern what is attended to and in what manner.

The major lessons on the nature of wisdom from the Berlin Wisdom Paradigm are that wisdom-related performance involves the synergistic interplay and coordination of multiple attributes, consists of organizing scripts around various criteria for understanding life, and can be cultivated under the right circumstances. Unfortunately, the research confirmed that people do not naturally become wise as they age and that most adults are not wise.[23]

Staudinger continued her work from the Berlin Wisdom Project and distinguished between general wisdom (i.e., understanding life as an observer, or from the balcony) and personal wisdom (i.e., personal maturity along with deep insight and meaning to one's own life). She documented that even though personal and general wisdom share parallel structures, they are also distinct constructs, far too evident when a parent advises a child to "do what I say" (general wisdom), "not what I do" (personal wisdom, or the lack thereof).[24] The Berlin Wisdom Paradigm provided a model for general wisdom. While the Berlin research had participants think out loud about problems involving fictitious people, the personal wisdom research had people "think out loud about yourself as a friend" when "solving a difficult and existential personal life problem."[25] The "as a friend" framing allowed participants to avoid the actor-observer bias (the tendency to focus on circumstances versus one's own characteristics and strategies when reflecting on personal dilemmas) and be more objective in their personal narratives. Staudinger noted that personal wisdom is more difficult to come by than general wisdom since the former requires reflective vulnerability with oneself and others about one's emotions and life choices.

The next major empirical model of wisdom emerged from Robert Sternberg. Reflecting on his forty-year career in higher education as a cognitive psychologist and researcher, Sternberg chronicled his study on intelligence, creativity, and wisdom, beginning with his seventh-grade science project on intelligence testing.[26] While at Yale University, Sternberg and his colleagues examined how people processed information and identified various components of intelligence (meta-components, performance components, and knowledge-acquisition components). In the early 1980s, Sternberg believed that there was still something more to intelligence than what was provided in his componential approach. Sternberg developed his triarchic theory of intelligence:

- Information-processing components (analysis)
- Creative and automated use of the intellectual process components (application of analysis to new situations)

• Practically applying the components to adapting, shaping, and/or selecting environments (analysis applied to everyday situations)

Sternberg observed that at this stage in his research, he "was viewing intelligence as some kind of weighted combination of its analytical, creative, and practical aspects, and that was wrong."[27] He observed that people can be Machiavellian, analytical, ruthlessly creative, and technically pragmatic, yet unethical and self-serving (e.g., scandals perpetuated by highly intelligent CEOs and dictators, etc.) and concluded that theories of successful intelligence were incomplete, including his own. He began to differentiate general intelligence from successful intelligence and concluded that

> people are intelligent, in large part, by virtue of recognizing their strengths and weaknesses, and of finding ways to capitalize on their strengths and compensating for or correcting their weakness. No single weighted combination of skills characterized a person's intelligence because people succeed in large part not just because of their abilities, but also because of their patterns of capitalization, on one hand, and compensation and correction, on the other.[28]

Sternberg then assessed approximately one thousand high school seniors and college freshmen to develop validated measures for creative and practical factors to complement the already-established measures on analytical factors. Applying the research across cultures, Sternberg realized that because of peoples' implicit theories of wisdom, they "could be plenty smart but remarkably foolish" because "book smart" and "street smart" were two different constructs.[29] At that point, Sternberg acknowledged that his "theory of successful intelligence lacked one crucial feature: It did not consider wisdom."[30] From that point on, he studied "wisdom as the application of the analytical, creative, and practical aspects of successful intelligence for a common good, over the long as well as the short terms, through the infusion of positive values."[31]

As a result of his cumulative psychometric testing of intelligence, creativity, and wisdom, Sternberg developed his balanced theory of wisdom that treats intelligence, creativity, and wisdom as different levels of understanding, with wisdom being the highest of the three, noting that while successful intelligence and creativity are necessary conditions for wisdom, they are not sufficient. According to Sternberg, there are intelligent people who lack creativity and creative people who lack wisdom.[32] Sternberg defined *wisdom* as the

> application of successful intelligence and creativity as mediated by values toward the achievement of a common good through a balance among (a) intrapersonal, (b) interpersonal, and (c) extrapersonal interests, over (a) short and (b) long terms, in order to achieve a balance among (a) adaptation to existing environments, (b) shaping of existing environments, and (c) selection of new environments.[33]

Sternberg later added that "an appropriate balance of interests, an appropriate response to the environment, and even the common good, all hinge on ethical values" and that "one cannot be personally wise without being ethical."[34] Sternberg astutely asked that "given that IQs have been rising, what does our world have to show for it?"[35] He lamented that "judging by the amount of seriousness and sheer scale of global conflict, perhaps not much. Certainly, there is no reason to believe that increasing IQs have improved people's or nations' relations with each other."[36] Sternberg emerged from his research a strong advocate that in addition to intelligence, education should focus on cultivating creativity and wisdom for success.

Intelligence, creativity, and expertise are related to wisdom, yet are distinct constructs. The more traditional definitions of intelligence dealt with intellectual abilities, the ability to acquire, process, and demonstrate mastery of specific content. The early definitions were limited to the various assessments used to measure so-called intelligence, tests such as the initial Stanford-Binet Intelligence Scales, the Scholastic Aptitude Test, and the Wechsler Intelligence Scale for Children, which saw intelligence as a uniform and fixed trait, in contrast to Robert Sternberg and Carol Dweck, who saw intelligence as socially constructed and malleable.[37] Sternberg defined *successful intelligence* as "the ability to achieve success in life in terms of one's personal standards, within one's sociocultural context."[38] According to Sternberg, successful intelligence has analytical, creative, and practical aspects. Building on the foundations of neuroscience research, Carol Dweck established that learners' beliefs about their intelligence or ability were significant to their actual performance.[39] In her widely disseminated work, *Mindset: The New Psychology of Success*, Dweck presented two mindsets: Fixed and Growth. People with a Growth Mindset believe that their abilities can be developed over time as the result of hard work, good instruction, and persistence.

The Cambridge Handbook of Creativity documented that creativity contains three features. "First, creative ideas must represent something different, new, or innovative. Second, creative ideas are of high quality. Third, creative ideas must also be appropriate to the task at hand, or some redefinition of that task. Thus, a creative response is novel, good, and relevant."[40] Creative thinking has been associated with divergent thinking in contrast to convergent thinking and defined as "the development of new mental patterns."[41]

Expertise is associated with having superior knowledge, understanding, and performance that distinguishes the expert from the rest of the crowd. *The Cambridge Handbook of Expertise and Expert Performance* documented that experts have advanced ways of understanding and mastering specific content and/or skills that set them apart.[42] Expertise requires not only knowledge of the content (i.e., a level of intelligence), but also a deeper level of understanding from a reflective study and practice that generates tacit depths of knowing. One can have a deep tacit and nuanced understanding of a phenomenon but still lack novel insights (creativity) on what are competing and ultimate considerations.

In his synthesis of wisdom, intelligence, and creativity, Sternberg concluded:

> the components of intelligence are at the base of successful intelligence, creativity, and wisdom. They are applied in intelligence, broadly defined, to experience in order to adapt to, shape, and select environments. When the components are involved in fairly abstract but familiar kinds of tasks, they are used analytically. When they are involved in relatively novel tasks and situations, they are used creatively. When they are involved in adaptation to, shaping of, and selection of environments, they are used practically.[43]

Intelligence is knowledge of the particulars and patterns, creativity is novel connections within and among the patterns, and wisdom is the ability to leverage the most appropriate pattern among many competing patterns at any given time.

Sternberg's Balance Model requires the wise to have a level of expertise on intrapersonal, interpersonal, and extrapersonal dynamics and their corresponding impact on the short- and long-term, supporting the findings of the Berlin Wisdom Project. As already stated, while intelligence, creativity, and expertise are related and overlapping concepts to wisdom, they are also distinct levels of knowing and understanding.[44]

Positive psychology focuses on strengths and wellness, or "why and how things go right," in response and in contrast to the traditional view of psychology, which focuses primarily on illness or "why and how things go wrong." Psychologists Martin Seligman and Christopher Peterson, cofounders of positive psychology, provided relevant insights on the nature of wisdom in their work on the psychology of traits associated with "the good life lived over time."[45] Following an extensive collection of data, their work culminated in a classification system of virtues and character strengths, outlined in their book, *Character Strengths and Virtues: A Handbook and Classification*.[46] This work was groundbreaking in that it provided a counternarrative to the existing classification system, the *Diagnostic and Statistical Manual of Mental Disorders* (DSM). Where the DSM is a necessary and useful tool when things go wrong, the strengths-based classification system provided the first of such tools from the lens of positive psychology—valuing both strengths and weaknesses. Moving beyond simply providing a classification system to expand basic knowledge, Peterson and Seligman also sought application, believing that strengths and virtues can and should be developed and cultivated:

> The classification of strengths presented in this book is intended to reclaim the study of character and virtue as legitimate topics of psychological inquiry and informed societal discourse. By providing ways of talking about character strengths and measuring them across the life span, this classification will start to make possible a science of human strengths that goes beyond armchair philosophy and political rhetoric. We believe that good character can be cultivated, but to do so, we need conceptual and empirical tools to craft and evaluate interventions.[47]

A cursory reading of positive psychology may lead the reader to conclude there is little contrast to the humanistic psychologies of the preceding decades. Though, as Peterson and Seligman pointed out, one crucial difference (though not the only difference) is the reliance on the collection of empirical data in support of positive psychology's cornerstones. While humanistic psychology was "unable to offer an alternative other than the insight that people were good,"[48] positive psychologists see both strengths and weaknesses as important and within the reach of scientific inquiry and understanding. Specifically, positive psychology aims to address:

> the study of positive subjective experiences, the study of positive individual traits, and the study of institutions that enable positive experiences and positive traits (Seligman & Csikszentmihalyi, 2000). Our classification project addresses the second of these topics and in so doing hopes to shed light on the first. One eventual benefit of the classification we propose may be the identification or even the deliberate creation of institutions that enable good character.[49]

Peterson and Seligman developed a system of six classes of virtues that are made up of twenty-four character strengths. Table 3.2 delineates and illustrates the virtues and strengths, as well as the corresponding relationships between the two.

Peterson and Seligman delineated the nuanced definitions and corresponding relationships among virtues, character strengths, and situational themes.

> Virtues are the core characteristics valued by moral philosophers and religious thinkers: wisdom, courage, humanity, justice, temperance, and transcendence. These six broad categories of virtue emerge consistently from historical surveys. . . . [T]hese are universal, perhaps grounded in biology through an evolutionary process that selected for these aspects of excellence as means of solving the important tasks necessary for survival of the species. We speculate that all these virtues must be present at above-threshold values for an individual to be deemed of good character.
>
> Character strengths are the psychological ingredients—processes or mechanisms—that define the virtues. Said another way, they are distinguishable routes to displaying one or another of the virtues. For example, the virtue of wisdom can be achieved through such strengths as creativity, curiosity, love of learning, open-mindedness, and what we call perspective—having a "big picture" on life. These strengths are similar in that they all involve the acquisition and use of knowledge, but they are also distinct. Again, we regard these strengths as ubiquitously recognized and valued, although a given individual will rarely, if ever, display all of them. We are comfortable saying that someone is of good character if he or she displays but 1 or 2 strengths within a virtue group.

Table 3.2. Virtues and Corresponding Character Strengths

Wisdom	Courage	Humanity	Justice	Temperance	Transcendence
Creativity	Bravery	Love	Citizenship	Forgiveness and Mercy	Appreciation of Beauty
Curiosity	Persistence	Kindness	Fairness	Humility and Modesty	Gratitude
Open-mindedness	Integrity	Social Intelligence	Leadership	Prudence	Hope
Love of Learning	Vitality			Self-regulation	Humor
Perspective					Spirituality

Situational themes are the specific habits that lead people to manifest given character strengths in given situations. . . . On a conceptual level, themes differ from character strengths in several crucial ways. First, they are thoroughly located in specific situations. . . may differ across cultures, cohorts, gender, and other important social contrasts. . . . Finally, themes per se are neither good nor bad; they can be used to achieve strengths and hence contribute to virtues, but they can also be harnessed to silly or wrong purposes.[50]

To develop the classification system, Peterson and Seligman gathered data through "brainstorming" and a dialogical process with notable scholars such as Donald Clifton, Mihaly Csikszentmihalyi, and Markus Buckingham.[51] In addition, they engaged in an exhaustive literature search for constructs and existing inventories associated with wisdom. Their inquiry was influenced by predecessors such as Eric Erickson and Howard Gardner,[52] as well as sources spanning across time and culture. For example, works by ancient philosophers and from religious texts were considered, as well as references to wisdom from popular culture—"virtue-relevant messages in Hallmark greeting cards, bumper stickers, *Saturday Evening Post* covers by Norman Rockwell, personal ads, popular song lyrics, graffiti, Tarot cards, the profiles of Pokémon characters, and the residence halls of Hogworts [*sic*]."[53] Due in part to the unique approach to data gathering, their resultant findings provided a foundation from which universals, transcending time and culture, could be sought. Peterson and Seligman described the final stages of the development of their system:

> When data collection was complete, analysis involved condensing each list by locating thematically similar virtues and classifying them under an obviously emerging core virtue. By that term, we mean an abstract ideal encompassing a number of other, more specific virtues that reliably converge to the recognizable higher-order category. For instance, the core virtue justice is an abstract term representative of the ideals of more minimalist virtues such as injunctions, laws, and procedural rules for fairness (see Bok, 1995, for further discussion on minimalist values and virtues). To say that particular virtues— within a tradition—converge into a core virtue is not to argue that all their features line up perfectly, but rather that they have a coherent resemblance to one another, sharing more features than not. Individual virtues that could not, without pushing and squeezing, be classified within a core virtue category

were considered distinct. Furthermore, to say that certain virtues—across traditions—converge onto a core virtue likewise does not mean that we argue for a one-to-one mapping of a virtue across cultures. Certainly an abstraction such as justice will mean slightly different things—and will be valued for different reasons—from one culture to another. Again what we suggest is coherent resemblance: The higher order meaning behind a particular core virtue will line up better with its cross-cultural counterpart than it will with any other core virtue (e.g., examples of Confucian justice will have more to do with those of Platonic justice than they will with Platonic wisdom). What we sought were instances in which the similarities across cultures outweighed the differences; again, when the core virtue of a particular tradition did not have an obvious cross-cultural counterpart, it was considered as a separate entity in the final analysis.[54]

Related specifically to this primer, the core virtue of wisdom calls for special attention. Peterson and Seligman described wisdom as a type of intelligence, though defined differently than IQ, stating, "It is knowledge, yes, but not reducible to the mere sum of books read, or lectures attended, or facts acquired. Perhaps it has something to do with living through hardship, emerging a better person able to share what has been learned with others."[55] As indicated in Table 3.2, their research identified five character strengths associated with wisdom:

- Creativity—original and novel insights,
- Curiosity—intrinsic openness to novel experiences,
- Open-mindedness—flexible and broad-minded critical thinking,
- Love of learning—vitality and motivation to acquire new knowledge and skills, and
- Perspective—empathetic and long-view understanding of life.

Interestingly, their nuancing of wisdom, as a virtue, drew from the philosophical tradition and the work of the Berlin Max Planck Institute, Erikson, and Sternberg. In the end, they described wisdom as "knowledge hard fought for, and then used for good."[56]

Peterson and Seligman building on both ancient and contemporary works formulated behaviorally defined and observable criterion that are amenable to reliable psychometric measurement and thus allow for application as an assessment. They described the specific assessment, the *Values in Action Inventory of Strengths (VIA-IS)* as:

> The assessment strategy we have most extensively developed to date entails self-report surveys able to be completed by respondents in a single session. We have devised separate inventories for adults and for young people (aged 10–17). Although our literature reviews concluded that some small number of the character strengths have not been and perhaps cannot be measured with self-report, we nonetheless attempted to create self-report scales for each of the 24 strengths.[57]

The empirical insights from the Berlin Wisdom Project, the Sternberg Balance Model of Wisdom, and Peterson and Seligman's Character Strengths and Virtues classification systems yielded cumbersome, albeit organic, models of wisdom. While each model is efficacious, they suffer from a common methodological limitation in empirical research in the social sciences. Reducing complex phenomena, such as wisdom, to measurable constructs can yield relatively arbitrary models, a kind of tautological quandary. Sternberg compared it to "putting the cart before the horse, defining the construct conceptually on the basis of how it is operationalized rather than vice versa."[58] Accordingly, "correlations among wisdom measures are surprisingly low, so the choice of a particular measure may strongly influence the study results."[59]

COMPLEXITY SCIENCE

Beginning in the 1940s, complexity theory emerged from research in both the physical and social sciences. Scientists from multiple disciplines discovered an underlying and hidden architecture that governed how and why the phenomena of their respective fields of study behaved the way they did. When the various scientists began to compare notes, they realized that all complex adaptive systems (CAS) were governed by the same set of rules.[60] Complexity science describes simply how nature works,[61] thereby providing a valuable meta-framework, or to use the terminology from the Berlin Wisdom Model, a metaheuristic to understand ubiquitous patterns in the universe at both the micro- and macro-levels. It provides a perspective-taking model, to use Peterson and Seligman's description of wisdom.

Richard Koch, in his critique of the traditional empirical method of knowing, observed that:

> The last third of the twentieth century has seen a revolution in the way that scientists think about the universe, overturning the prevailing wisdom of the past 350 years. That prevailing wisdom was a machine-based and rational view. . . . All phenomena were reduced to predictable, *linear* relationships. . . . But in the second half of the twentieth century it seems much more accurate to view the world as an evolving organism where the whole system is more than the sum of its parts, and where relationship between parts are nonlinear. Causes are difficult to pin down, there are complex interdependencies between causes and causes and effects are blurred. The snag with linear thinking is that it doesn't always work, it is an oversimplification of reality. Equilibrium is illusory or fleeting. The universe is wonky.[62]

Koch concluded, "Yet chaos theory [complexity theory], despite its name, does not say that everything is a hopeless and incomprehensible mess. Rather, there is a self-organized logic lurking behind the disorder, a predictable nonlinearity."[63]

John Shoup and Susan Studer provided in their book, *Leveraging Chaos: The Mysteries of Leadership and Policy Revealed*, a brief history of complexity science and detailed descriptions and examples of seven features common to all dynamic systems. They demonstrated that complexity science provides a lens for recognizing patterns and leverage points to better manage complex systems of all sorts. They noted that "leaders who understand the rules that govern dynamic social systems are skilled enough in the nuances of the systems to lead with wisdom—leading from the metanarrative or big picture."[64] Complexity science provides a framework or lens to exercise practical wisdom by discerning the respective root reasons and solutions that govern optimal functioning of CAS in the natural and social worlds. All dynamic systems have seven common features and explain why and how dynamic systems function, survive, and even thrive at the edge of chaos. The seven elements are: (a) homeostasis and change, (b) strange attractors, (c) feedback, (d) fractals, (e) emergence, (f) sensitive dependence, and (g) self-organized criticality.

CAS make ongoing corrections (change) to sustain stability (homeostasis) and grow (emergence). One of the more basic systems, albeit complex, is the human body. The human body continually sends and monitors messages (feedback) to maintain a desired balance (homeostasis) within and among its different biological systems for the body to thrive (equilibrium) and adjust (emergence). For example, the body regulates its own temperature to protect it from over- and underheating around the desired equilibrium point (or strange attractor) of 98.6°F (37°C). When the hypothalamus detects that the body is getting too hot or too cold, it triggers:

- minute muscles to have the hairs on the skin either stand (to reduce heat loss) or lie flat (increase heat loss);
- blood vessels to widen (to bring heat to the surface) or constrict (to keep the body warmer on the inside); and/or
- glands to secrete sweat to increase heat loss by evaporation.

Each biological system (respiratory, digestive, circulatory, renal, endocrine, nervous, musculoskeletal, exocrine, lymphatic, and reproductive) in the human body interacts with the others to maintain an overall balance, consistently making necessary adjustments so that all systems can function at optimal levels. Each system maintains a pattern around desired equilibrium points (e.g., body temperature, heart rate, cell chemistry, etc.). Each equilibrium point serves as the reference (i.e., strange attractor) for what is an acceptable range of tolerance before the system triggers a change to self-correct. The collection of systems also maintains patterns around multiple reference points (i.e., strange attractors) to keep the whole system functioning (e.g., diet, exercise, and sleep patterns) in relative equilibrium.

Social systems, like physical systems, have their own "strange attractors" (i.e., equilibrium points and ranges of tolerance around competing values) and feedback mechanisms to manage change and maintain relative homeostasis. For example, the American election system is characterized by competitive and partisan cycles. A long view of American presidential elections reveals a pattern in which no one party has been in office for more than eight years, on average, since 1856.[65] The alternating party victories are how the system changes periodically to maintain balance between the two sets of competing and relevant party agendas over time. Each political party serves as a corrective to the other, such that overall, the system maintains relative balance of policies around America's dominant values (i.e., strange attractors) of life, liberty, and the pursuit of happiness (*eudaimonia*). The more subsystems within a system, the greater the complexity. Mayors of small towns provide comprehensive services to a diverse set of constituents by balancing competing priorities with limited resources. Serving as the mayor of a large city is a bit more complicated than the service of the mayor of a small town. Serving as a county executive officer requires balancing even more interrelated parts, as he or she must oversee multiple incorporated and unincorporated cities and towns. Serving as a state governor is even more complex, given the governor serves an even larger and more diverse group of constituents, including a plethora of towns, cities, and counties. At one level, a mayor deals with the same issues and challenges as a state governor and needs similar leadership abilities, but at different scales (e.g., fractals). To govern wisely, elected officials balance layers of competing expectations and demands to keep their system in relative equilibrium in relation to overlapping systems.

The etymology and function of a "governor" provide a direct parallel between complexity science and the wisdom literature.

Cybernetics is the word of choice for feedback among complexity aficionados. Cybernetics, while used by Plato, was popularized by Norbert Weiner in 1948 with his book, *Cybernetics.* Plato and Ampere (1834) used the term to discuss the science of government and the activity of the "governor" as steering the community. Wiener used the metaphor of cybernetics to describe communication and control of animals and machines.

The word *cybernetics* is a transliteration of the Greek word Κυβερνήτης (*kubernites*) and literally means steersman. The individual staffing the rudder of a ship is constantly making minor midcourse corrections to keep the ship headed toward its destination; the more the steersman adjusts the rudder (change) the better able to stay the course (remain the same). Just as the stronger currents or winds require the steersman to make more changes, complex environments require skilled steersman to respond to the many competing demands.[66]

Governing is a form of fine-tuning, monitoring, and implementing corrective and adaptive changes for the system to survive and thrive. Discerning what and how much fine-tuning is needed, not wanting to over- or under-correct, is the heart of governing wisely.

Some variables in CAS are sensitively dependent on others and critically self-organized, meaning that a change in one variable can cause a greater chain reaction than others, and the extent of that chain reaction is a function of proximity and timing of the precipitating change. In other words, systems have unique tipping points that make and remake them.

Sensitive dependence on initial conditions, also known as the "butterfly effect," explains how and why initial conditions and some small changes have disproportionate impacts on individual and overlapping systems. The *butterfly effect* is a term coined by MIT mathematician and meteorologist Edward Lorenz in the early 1960s after experimenting with computers to predict weather. On one occasion, he began his weather simulation program at the midpoint, using previous calculated values for that point in the data run, and he derived a drastically different and unexpected result compared to when he entered the original start data at the front end of the calculations. After ruling out a computer malfunction, Lorenz concluded that the extremely minor change of rounding decimals to their nearest thousandth value was the equivalent of a butterfly flapping its wings in Brazil and setting off a tornado in Texas.[67]

The QWERTY keyboard is a classic example of how and why initial conditions matter in CAS. The strikers on the initial manual typewriters would get stuck when the keys were pressed too fast. A set of frequently used letters were reassigned to the upper left side of the keyboard creating the QWERTY configuration. The new placement of the letters generated slower typing speeds and subsequently fewer stuck typebars. The advent of the electronic typewriter eliminated the need for manual strikers and opened the door for a new keyboard configuration that facilitated faster typing speeds. The slower QWERTY keyboard was retained to avoid a major disruption that would require people to relearn how they typed. The butterfly effect also explains how and why encouraging words and acts of kindness can turn a bad day into a good day, how enthusiastic teachers can alter good students' academic trajectories, and how bad leaders can ruin good people and organizations just as simply as good leaders can help people and organizations thrive.

Self-organized criticality is the principle behind the old adages of "the straw that broke the camel's back" and "no one snowflake is responsible for an avalanche." It really was not the last straw or snowflake, but the cumulative effect of everything else at a particular time that caused the camel's back to collapse or the avalanche to occur. Dense interdependent connections create critical states. The same conditions that trigger minor earthquakes and avalanches are also responsible for major earthquakes and avalanches. While the latter are proportionately less rare, the former occasionally cause a cascade of like events of various greater magnitudes.

It is the timing and relationship of the variables to one another in CAS that determines specific tipping points: from when a small earthquake triggers a major earthquake, a fluctuation in the stock market becomes a recession, a family argument turns violent, a peaceful protest converts to a riot, and a regional military skirmish escalates to war. Self-organized criticality explains how and why the shot fired in a skirmish in Lexington, Massachusetts, between British troops and American colonists became the "shot heard around the world" and triggered the American Revolution, and Rosa Parks's refusal to change seats on a bus was a catalyst to the American civil rights movement. CAS exist, and some would say thrive, at the edge of relative chaos. Self-organized criticality is the reason that people should plan for the best and prepare for the worst, knowing that occasionally CAS will encounter periods of crises.

Axiomatic to sensitive dependency on initial conditions and self-organized criticality is how and why the root cause of events and behaviors is often several layers deep within CAS. Taiichi Ohno was a Japanese industrial engineer who pioneered Toyota's Total Production Systems in the 1950s and developed the 5-Why Process based upon his knowledge of complex systems. Ohno documented that it typically takes "five whys" to get to the root cause of a problem, often illustrated in his more popular example:

1. *Why* did the machine stop?
   There was an overload, and the fuse blew.

2. *Why* was there an overloaded?
   The bearing was not sufficiently lubricated.

3. *Why* was it not lubricated sufficiently?
   The oil pump on the robot is not circulating sufficient oil.

4. *Why* was it not pumping sufficiently?
   The shaft of the pump was worn and rattling.

5. *Why* was the shaft worn out?
   There was no strainer attached and metal scrap got in.[68]

If a governor's discernment in evaluating the source of a particular problem stopped at the proximate causes prior to the root cause, he or she might just keep replacing fuses or oil. As Ohno stated, "By asking *why* five times and answering it each time, we can get to the real cause of the problem, which is often hidden behind more obvious symptoms."[69]

Complexity science's connection to the wisdom literature is its ability to provide insights on how nature really works. Specifically, all CAS are relatively stable patterns of interactions around desired equilibrium points (i.e., strange attractors) that naturally mirror themselves throughout respective subsystems (i.e., fractals). The patterns emerged over time based upon initial conditions and ongoing self-corrections (i.e., change) to feedback. While relatively stable, CAS are vulnerable to tipping points (self-organized criticality) that periodically disrupt and change the system. Discerning the patterns and logic governing the various patterns equips governors to optimize individual and collective performance, and hence to live and lead wisely by judiciously attending to and leveraging each feature of all CAS. Complexity science provides the language and framework to understand the logic and true nature of reality lurking below the surface.

CONCLUSION

The construct of wisdom is elusive because it deals with judgment about what is right and the better things to do in the affairs of life. Ardelt demonstrated that wisdom has cognitive, reflective, and affective dimensions. Baltes and his colleagues documented that wisdom can be considered a level of expertise on the fundamental pragmatics of life. Sternberg argued that wisdom is balancing the short- and long-term intrapersonal, interpersonal, and extrapersonal interests. Peterson and Seligman posited that wisdom consists of several strengths that facilitate higher forms of perspective-taking.

Table 3.3. Synthesis of Empirical Wisdom Models

Ardelt's Three-Dimensional Personality Model of Wisdom	Baltes's Expert Theory of Wisdom	Sternberg's Balance Theory of Wisdom	Peterson & Seligman's Virtues and Character Strengths	Complexity Science (Systems Theory of Wisdom)
Cognitive and Reflective	Rich Factual Knowledge Rich Procedural Knowledge	Application of Tacit Knowledge	Love of Learning	Knowledge of Systems Logic
Reflective and Affective	Lifespan Contextualism	Balancing Intrapersonal, Interpersonal, and Extrapersonal Interests	Curiosity and Creativity	Homeostasis, Change, Sensitive Dependence, and Self-organized Criticality
Reflective, Affective, and Cognitive	Value Relativism	Mediated by Values	Perspective-taking	Competing Strange Attractors
Reflective and Cognitive	Management of Uncertainty	Adapting to and Shaping Existing Environments, and Selecting New Environments	Open-mindedness	Homeostasis, Change, Emergence, Self-organized Criticality, and Tolerance of Complexity

Complexity science, while not an explicit theory on wisdom, demonstrates how the fundamental pragmatics of life emerge and maintain relative equilibrium around cherished values (strange attractors). The empirical tradition on wisdom is limited to the pragmatics of life, in part because of its methodology of addressing only what can be observed and measured, and it does not address *sophia* as nuanced in the philosophical and theological traditions.

As illustrated in Table 3.3, the Ardelt, Baltes, Sternberg, Peterson and Seligman, and complexity science models of wisdom have much conceptual overlap. All five models identify the need to manage the relative indeterminacy of life, as well as ways to manage one's environment. While Ardelt's cognitive and reflective dimensions of wisdom have explicit overlap with the other four models, her affective dimension is not overt in the other four models, even though there are loose references.

The five empirical models, like the theological and philosophical traditions, recognize that knowledge is a precursor to understanding, and that understanding is a precursor to wisdom. The models acknowledge that wisdom is needed to navigate and balance competing values and demands for both short- and long-term considerations. Wisdom is a metaheuristic based upon a level of expertise that uniquely frames problems and solutions to discern how to dynamically balance "everything" in complex adaptive systems. It ultimately involves the identification and balanced pursuit of the more virtuous ends and means. Each model is restricted to observations in the natural world and therefore is limited to practical wisdom, in contrast to the *sophia* wisdom that is associated with ultimate truth and values as highlighted in the philosophical and theological traditions.

REFLECTION AND DISCUSSION QUESTIONS

1. What are implicit and explicit approaches to the study of wisdom, and how do they complement each other?
2. What are the key features of Ardelt's, Baltes's, and Sternberg's models of wisdom, and what do they have in common?
3. How is wisdom different from intelligence and creativity?

4. How has positive psychology changed the study of human behavior and added to the study of wisdom?
5. Why and how is complexity theory a metaheuristic for gaining wisdom?
6. Why and how does the governing metaphor capture the essence of how CAS function and prove useful for leading collectives wisely?
7. What does complexity theory have in common with the wisdom models proposed by Ardelt, Baltes, Sternberg, and Peterson and Seligman?
8. What are some of the limitations of the empirical models of wisdom and their corresponding solutions?

4

THE NATURE OF WISDOM

A Model to Understand, Acquire, Practice, and Teach Wisdom

A newly licensed nurse is working in an emergency room when it is suddenly swarmed with patients with varying levels of trauma from a multi-vehicle accident. All medical personnel are in triage mode when the primary doctor tells the novice nurse to administer a particular intravenous drip (IV) to a specific patient. The nurse recalls from her recent learning that the drug prescribed by the doctor is contraindicated and would be fatal given the condition of the patient. She expresses her concern to the doctor, who, in turn, asserts his authority and reiterates the order as he races off to tend to the other patients. The nurse is left alone to implement a consequential decision that goes against her novice professional judgment.

The nurse is now facing a dilemma. She naturally second-guesses her professional judgment given her rookie status and the doctor's authority and experience. It would be easy in the frenetic work environment to ignore the dilemma and defer to the doctor. If her original assessment proves correct and the patient dies, however, the nurse will live with the regret and guilt over what could have been an avoidable tragedy if she had spoken up. If she administers the drug and the patient lives, she finds relief in being wrong, but she is not necessarily absolved of the guilt associated with implementing a decision that went against her conscience. If the nurse refuses to comply with the doctor, she risks losing her coveted job and becoming branded as "the nurse who does not follow doctors' orders," likely never to be hired again. Should the nurse implement the doctor's orders or not? How would you advise the nurse in the heat of the moment?

Fortunately, in this real-life scenario, the nurse demonstrated wisdom in her words, demeanor, and behavior to act in a manner that honored the doctor, the patient, the profession, and herself, while navigating the uncertainty of who was right. Prior to revealing what the nurse did, this chapter synthesizes the learning from the previous chapters to provide a model of the nature of wisdom. The model provides a simple framework to understand, acquire, teach, and practice general wisdom. The chapter offers several examples that illustrate the nature of wisdom, including what the nurse did in the scenario outlined above. But first, a brief excursus on the nature of truth, the foundation for understanding and practicing wisdom.

TRUTH AND RIGHTNESS

The pursuit of wisdom in the philosophical, theological, and empirical traditions is ultimately about what is true and right, in contrast to what is not or less true and right. The assumption common to all three traditions is that people want and need the truth if they are to be skilled at living. Truth is what makes wisdom possible. So, what is truth?

Truth is the nature of reality. There are two types of reality—objective and subjective. Objective reality exists independent of the interpreter—the state of Minnesota exists; Abraham Lincoln was the sixteenth president; a criminal defendant is either guilty or innocent of a crime; and a true God either exists or does not exist. Subjective reality is based upon social framing and is contingent upon the interpreters' values and biases—Minnesota is nice place to live; Abraham Lincoln was the best president; the crime is or is not a big deal, or the minimum or maximum sentencing should be rendered; and people should or should not seek the true God. There is one objective reality, often referred to as *Truth* with a big *T*. There are multiple subjective realities, often referred to as *truths* with a small *t*.[1]

How do people know the Truth and the truth? How do people know whether their conclusions align with the nature of reality? Ultimately, knowledge of reality is based upon the interpretation and understanding of the facts at hand. For example, how do people know that Abraham Lincoln was the sixteenth president, decide who was the best president, render a correct verdict in a jury trial, and confirm God's existence and nature? The statement from the original Superman series, "Look, in the sky, it's a bird, no—it's a plane, no—it's Superman," reveals much about the relationship between metaphysics and epistemology. Metaphysically, the item in question can only be a bird, a plane, or Superman (or even something else for that matter). The nature of reality requires that it be a distinct object. How we know what that distinct reality is, is related to epistemology. It is very accurate to state that some conclusions about the nature of reality are more accurate than others—it is a bird, or a plane, or Superman, but it is not all three at the same time. In other words, metaphysically speaking, facts are objective. Epistemologically speaking, facts are subjective.

A telling example of the relationship between metaphysics and epistemology is the classic poem based upon a Hindu parable, *The Parable of the Blind Men and the Elephant* by John Godfrey Saxe.[2] Six blind "scientists" approach different parts of the elephant and begin to compare notes. Each has a different conclusion: It is like a wall; a spear; a snake; a tree; a fan; and a rope. Given their unique experience with the empirical data (epistemology), they spend the next several minutes debating the object in question (metaphysics) and how the others could be so wrong in their interpretation of the data. Like the blind scientists, people go through life making definitive conclusions about the nature of reality without knowing what they do not know and/or not realizing that their inferences may be incomplete. Lacking omniscience, people possess partial information when making inferences about the nature of reality, which presents a second, and often paradoxical element to epistemology.

For many people, there is a misguided perception of a dichotomy between the exercise of faith and reason. Demystifying the word faith addresses one of the epistemological concerns of knowing truth. Because faith is often associated with theological truths, the concept typically takes on a mystical tone, often contrasted with reason. Many people assume that for faith to be "faith," it must be blind, void of any reason, as if people should not be able to explain why they believe what they believe. However, the process of faith is very rational. At the same time, almost every rational statement and resulting behavior has an element of faith, from the chairs people sit in, to the airplanes they board, to the people they marry, and to the gods they choose to serve.

Faith alone will not keep a defective chair from collapsing, make an airplane with a broken wing fly, turn a philanderer into a faithful spouse, or animate an idol such that it becomes an all-loving, omniscient, omnipotent, and omnipresent god. In the same way, reason alone will not guarantee a sturdy chair from breaking, prevent a new plane from malfunctioning, keep a faithful spouse from cheating, or justify obeying a god's counterintuitive commands.

Lacking omniscience, the best people can do with every belief is to exercise faith based on the most reasonable judgments at the time. Cybernetic epistemology, the hermeneutical spiral, and the nature of scientific revolutions demonstrate the process of validation and invalidation in discovering the truth, revealing the relationship between faith and reason.[3] The scientific method is one of repeated testing to correct and refine beliefs. Informed assumptions realign to what is known, later becoming the basis for future faith commitments, only to be validated or invalidated, causing informed assumptions to realign, accordingly, and become the basis for subsequent assumptions. That faith appealed to reason is revealed by two different epistemological statements made by the apostle Paul. In 2 Corinthians 15:1–17, Paul cited evidence for Christ's resurrection and explicitly stated that if Christ had not risen from the dead, then the Christian faith is worthless. Paul appealed to evidence to justify faith in Christ. In 2 Timothy 1:12, Paul expressed, "I know whom I have believed and I am convinced." Paul's act of believing caused him to obey God, resulting in him experiencing God's faithfulness, which resulted in Paul being convinced that he could trust God, causing him to obey all the more, and so on.

Since the act of knowing involves both faith and reason at various levels, is it possible to be certain and correct in our knowledge of the truth? Certainty and accuracy in interpretations are achieved when conclusions have been repeatedly validated and provide a comprehensive, congruent, consistent, cohesive, and verifiable explanation for the phenomena in question.[4] Going back to the six blind "scientists," each one had a faith statement based upon a reasonable interpretation of the available evidence. Through dialogue, they hoped to discern the nature of reality given their individual perceptions, and eventually, with additional information, they captured the essence of reality when they correctly identified the object as an elephant and all the parts of the puzzle fit neatly together.

Since beliefs are always open to corrections, beliefs about the nature of reality must be held relatively tentative with different degrees of confidence and certainty. For example, most adults are convinced that the earth orbits around the sun, as the compelling evidence leaves little room for doubt. However, prior to Nicolaus Copernicus (1473–1543) and Galileo Galilei (1564–1642), the prevailing belief was that the earth was the center of the universe. It is possible to attain certainty in beliefs, but it requires one to remain tentative in their conclusions, knowing that additional enlightenment may always be forthcoming to give additional meaning to the known facts, as illustrated in the history of scientific revolutions.[5] Beliefs are, at their best, reasonable faith propositions and convictions about the nature of reality.

Metaphysics, epistemology, and axiology are the categories that Western philosophers have developed to explore the dynamic nature and relationship of truth, knowing truth, and applying truth. The synthesized questions and answers to such deep and broad topics are what form people's beliefs and worldviews. *Worldview* is shorthand for the metaphysical, epistemological, and axiological assumptions and answers people have internalized and use to make subsequent interpretations of reality. Philosophers J. P. Moreland and William Lane Craig defined *worldview* as "an ordered set of propositions one believes, especially propositions about life's most important questions."[6] While there are different worldviews, all worldviews have a similar goal and address similar questions.[7] Everyone has a frame of reference on the who, what, when, how, and why questions of life. The mind needs a context to seek and make sense of its existence and environment. Worldviews are personal schematics that "help people simplify, effectively manage, and make sense of information in their surrounding environments and guide the cognition, interpretation, and ways of understanding events or objects."[8]

People vary to the degree in which they can articulate the assumptions and logic of their respective worldviews. People have unidentified, unevaluated, or evaluated assumptions about the nature of reality and knowing reality. While worldviews are at times incomplete, inconsistent, incohesive, and/or unverified, it is only through ongoing examination that people can develop accurate and reliable worldviews. Hence, the wisdom of Socrates that the examined life is worth living because it is then that people gain insight on the nature of reality.[9] The good news is that truth and corresponding beliefs can withstand scrutiny, and it is by scrutiny that beliefs become refined and eventually align with truth.

The foray into the nature of truth and knowing truth demonstrates that the best people can do in this temporal framework is to make the most reasonable inferences about the nature of reality and then live their lives in a manner consistent with those beliefs, making midcourse corrections when they bump into reality. People are expected to grow in knowledge and understanding, to have their conclusions continuously refined until they correspond with the nature of reality. As a result, knowing truth and practicing wisdom involve different combinations of humility, confidence, faith, and reason regarding truth claims and corresponding judgments.

Worldview is a metaheuristic that not only involves understanding the nature of truth and knowing the truth, but the content and process of making enlightened judgment calls on what is right and good. Axiology is the branch of philosophy that deals with the nature of values, goodness, and beauty. It explores the ethics and aesthetics of life. It asserts claims about what is good, better, and best in the realm of subjective truths predicated on objective truths. Typical questions include what makes something good and beautiful and what makes something better or more beautiful than others. While it might be easy to suggest that such questions are subjective, axiology reveals that certain criteria exist to provide some objective measure. This is evidenced in the fact that almost all people would say that the virtues are better habits than the vices. The field of axiology also recognizes that value judgments depend on one's worldview. Discerning (epistemology) what is right, good, and lovely is contextual to what is ultimately true (metaphysics) and one's understanding of such truth (epistemology).

Going back to the nurse and doctor scenario, the prescribed medicine will have a healing, fatal, or neutral effect on the patient. While they both want what is best for the patient (axiology), only one outcome is possible, albeit unknown at the front end of the decision (metaphysics). Unfortunately, the doctor and nurse have reached different inferences on the efficacy of the prescribed medicine (epistemology). They are both making faith claims about the outcome based upon their reasonable understanding of the facts.

Truth is what makes wisdom possible. The quest for truth and the right application of truth makes wisdom necessary. Wisdom is both the search for

THE NATURE OF WISDOM

and the outcome of worldviews with cohesive, consistent, comprehensive, congruent, and affirmable metaphysical, epistemological, and axiological conclusions.

SYNTHESIS: THE NATURE OF WISDOM

Philosophy treats wisdom as both an intellectual and a moral virtue based upon nuanced theoretical and practical understandings of life, typically acquired by sound reasoning and virtuous habits. It focuses on optimizing human flourishing by aligning choices with the ultimate and immediate *teloses* of life and particular situations. Theology treats wisdom as enlightened understandings and behaviors based upon the knowledge of the divine revealed in sacred texts. Its focus is on being skilled at living in the temporal world in light of eternal truths. The empirical tradition treats wisdom as having expert levels of understandings of the pragmatics of life and successfully navigating competing values and priorities to live ethically. The focus is balancing intrapersonal, interpersonal, and extrapersonal considerations for optimal functioning. All three traditions acknowledge that there are perpetual truths and patterns that govern reality, and that wisdom rightly discerns reality and correspondingly aligns choices, beliefs, dispositions, and habits with outcomes that will optimize human flourishing.

In conclusion, wisdom is a virtue that equips its possessors to be exceptionally skilled at living. It is an evaluative endeavor predicated on higher levels of understanding of the temporal and eternal realities that, in turn, yield insights to the multiple storylines at work in the universe. The type of storylines at work for general wisdom are identified in the previous chapters. Wisdom is judiciously balancing the visible and invisible truths and storylines associated with temporal and eternal realities and deferring to those that make the right and better things happen the right and better way.

Axiomatically, there are two types of wisdom. *Sophia* is wisdom associated with big *T* Truth, while *phronesis* is wisdom associated with small *t* truth. The two types of wisdom are two sides of the same coin. As a result, they are frequently used interchangeably because of such a tight and necessary connection. *Sophia* focuses on what is ultimately true and of better value.

Phronesis, or prudence, deals with what is most appropriate and beneficial among competing options given what is ultimately true and of better value.

EXAMPLES OF WISDOM

The following eleven examples illustrate the nature of wisdom as just described—discerning multiple storylines and patterns and aligning choices, beliefs, dispositions, and habits to the more noble and transcendent ones that promote human flourishing, those that lead to better outcomes and demonstrate advanced skills at living. The first three examples are from the Bible, the next four are from judicial and legal settings, and the remaining four are personal vignettes.

Proverbs 15:1 states that "a gentle word turns away wrath, but a harsh word stirs up anger" and presents two responses to perceived injustices. One option is to respond with a harsh word, increasing the probability of escalating the conflict. The other option is to respond with a tender answer, increasing the probability of deescalating the conflict. Prudence suggests responding with a gentle word is of greater benefit, like the expression that one can "catch more flies with honey than vinegar." *Sophia* recognizes that the quality of relationships often takes priority over the issue at hand, therefore giving way to responses that treat people with dignity, regardless of the situation, and choosing a more opportune time to deal with the instigating issue.

The nature of wisdom is revealed in the seemingly contradictory advice found in Proverbs 26:4–5. The wise are told "to not answer a fool according to their folly, lest you be like him" (verse 4), and yet they are told to "answer a fool as his folly deserves, that he not be wise in his own eyes" (verse 5). It is now a matter of prudence as to when and how to respond to a fool. If the fool is somewhat teachable, as implied in verse 5, then a proper reply is warranted. If the fool is only engaging to be argumentative, as implied in verse 4, then silence is the better response.

The most well-known example of administrative wisdom comes from King Solomon, who ruled Israel from 971 to 931 B.C.E. He was known for having such great wisdom that even foreign dignitaries traveled from afar to "hear the wisdom of Solomon" (1 Kings 4:34). On one occasion,

Solomon decided to split a baby in half. The story is revealed in 1 Kings 3:16–28:

> When two women who were harlots came to the king and stood before him. The one woman said, "Oh, my lord, this woman and I live in the same house; and I gave birth to a child while she was in the house. It happened on the third day after I gave birth, that this woman also gave birth to a child, and we were together. There was no stranger with us in the house, only the two of us in the house. This woman's son died in the night, because she lay on it. So she arose in the middle of the night and took my son from beside me while your maidservant slept, and laid him in her bosom, and laid her dead son in my bosom. When I rose in the morning to nurse my son, behold, he was dead; but when I looked at him carefully in the morning, behold, he was not my son, whom I had borne." Then the other woman said, "No! For the living one is my son, and the dead one is your son." But the first woman said, "No! For the dead one is your son, and the living one is my son." Thus they spoke before the king.
>
> Then the king said, "The one says, 'This is my son who is living, and your son is the dead one'; and the other says, 'No! For your son is the dead one, and my son is the living one.'" The king said, "Get me a sword." So they brought a sword before the king. The king said, "Divide the living child in two, and give half to the one and half to the other." Then the woman whose child was the living one spoke to the king, for she was deeply stirred over her son and said, "Oh, my lord, give her the living child, and by no means kill him." But the other said, "He shall be neither mine nor yours; divide him!" Then the king said, "Give the first woman the living child, and by no means kill him. She is his mother." When all Israel heard of the judgment which the king had handed down, they feared the king, for they saw that the wisdom of God was in him to administer justice.

When a mother loses an infant, it raises the question why bad things happen and brings to the forefront that life at times is unfair. King Solomon recognized that life is not always fair and the desire for justice is universal. The mourning mother, in her grief, sought some consolation and sense of justice in her loss by taking another's child. It was this sense of justice that Solomon tapped in to when he rendered a "fair" verdict to split the baby. At the same time, Solomon recognized that the maternal instinct was much more powerful, which also, in part, explained the grieving mother's selfish act. Solomon knew that the maternal instinct storyline trumped the deep grief associated with the loss of one's own infant and that the biological mother in this case would rather suffer an injustice to let her son live, even if it meant losing him. Hence, Solomon recognized three storylines at work in this scenario: life/death, justice, and maternal instinct. He cleverly tapped in to all three, knowing that the motherly love storyline would eclipse the other storylines and reveal the real mother of the living child. Another judge lacking Solomon's wisdom might have defaulted to possession as the rule of law and awarded custody to the wrong mother, while another might have awarded joint custody, emphasizing distributive justice at the expense of the more important consideration.

A modern example of wisdom and the lack of wisdom in a judicial setting comes from Barry Schwartz and Kenneth Sharpe, in their book, *Practical Wisdom: The Right Way to Do the Right Thing.*[10] The story begins with Michael appearing before a judge for robbing a taxi driver at gunpoint. "Shortly before the holdup Michael had lost his job. Despondent because he could not support his family, he went out on a Saturday night, had more than a few drinks, and then robbed the taxi."[11] The judge, Lois Forer, learning that Michael brandished a toy gun and that this was his first offense, exercised her discretion and sentenced Michael to "eleven and a half months in the county jail" and permitted "him to work outside the prison during the day to support his family."[12] Unfortunately, the prosecutor appealed the decision, and two years later the Pennsylvania Supreme Court ordered Judge Forer to resentence Michael to the mandatory minimum five years, even though sentencing guidelines allowed judges to deviate from prescribed sentences if mitigating circumstances existed. To make matters more tragic, in the interim, Michael had successfully completed his sentence under Judge Forer's terms, paid restitution to the taxi driver, and obtained steady employment. Rather than violate her conscience, Judge Forer resigned her position, and another judge sentenced Michael to the mandated sentence. The rigid-letter-of-the-law prosecutor and the Pennsylvania Supreme Court violated the spirit of the law and in their quest for justice created an additional injustice, at least in the judgment of Lois Forer, Barry Schwartz, Kenneth Sharpe, and the authors of this primer.

Another example of wisdom is found in the Constitution of the United States, itself born out of a wise process, as alluded to in a portion of a speech from the senior stateman in the room, Benjamin Franklin, at the conclusion of the Constitutional Convention on September 17, 1787. While acknowledging that a perfect constitution for a general government is not possible, Franklin observed:

> I doubt, too, whether any other Convention we can obtain, may be able to make a better Constitution: for when you assemble a number of men, to have the advantage of their joint wisdom, you inevitably assemble with those men, all their prejudices, their passions, their errors of opinion, their local interests, and their selfish views. From such an assembly can a perfect production be expected? It therefore astonishes me, Sir, to find this system approaching so near to perfection as it does; and I think it will astonish our enemies. . . .[13]

Securing the unanimous support of thirty-nine delegates[14] from twelve relatively diverse states is a testimony to the nature of wisdom and the fruit of wisdom. Founded on "reflection and choice" rather than on "accident and force," the U.S. Constitution has sustained a "republic based on the equality and consent of a self-governing people" over two centuries, despite periods of turmoil and corruption.[15]

The wisdom of the U.S. Constitution is eloquently documented by Michael and Luke Paulsen in their book, *The Constitution: An Introduction*. They elaborated on four cornerstones of the Constitution's "superstructure" and overall design that sets it apart: "First, the fact that it is a *written* constitution; second, its essentially *republic* character; third, the carefully crafted *separation of powers* among the branches of the national government; and fourth, the distinctive feature of *federalism*, dividing power between the national government and the states."[16] The Constitution captures the essence of *sophia* by becoming *the supreme Law of the Land* (Article VI), and as such becomes the final authority that binds each branch of government and the states to its enumerated powers. While the Constitution is open to interpretation, as a written text, the Constitution is used to interpret the Constitution. As a result, it is a self-referencing, stable, and enduring script to "establish Justice, ensure domestic Tranquility, provide for the general Welfare, and secure the Blessings of Liberty" for posterity (Preamble). As such, the U.S. Constitution is America's enduring "sacred" text to serve as the transcendent go-to narrative for governing in the United States.[17]

As noted in the Gettysburg Address, the republican form of government in the Constitution created a government "of the people, by the people, for the people."[18] While the Constitution is the supreme law of the land, it is the people who ultimately rule, not government officials. The Constitution precludes the appointment of nobility at the national and state levels (Article 1, Section 9, Clause 8 and Section 10, Clause 1, respectively). Furthermore, Article IV, Section 4 guarantees "every State in the Union a Republican Form of Government."[19] The *sophia* and *phronesis* of the republican Constitution is letting the will of the people ultimately rule through a duly elected and representative government.

The separation of powers and federalism wisely balance the distribution of political power among the three independent branches of government and between the national and state governments. The checks and balance in the separation of clearly enumerated powers reflects a *sophia* understanding of the nature of reality borne out in history—power tends to corrupt; hence "no branch is the boss of any of the others; none can tell the others what they *must* do. Rather, each branch is co-equal (or 'co-ordinate') under the Constitution."[20] That members of each branch are separately elected or appointed provides a prudent process to maintain separation of powers.

Additionally, the Constitution checks factions, or interest groups, that might seek to overwhelm other interest groups (e.g., large states versus small states, rural versus urban interests, etc.). The sticky wicket is doing so without violating the individual liberties sought to be protected. As James Madison wrote in Federalist No. 10, "There are again two methods of removing the causes of faction: the one, by destroying the liberty which is essential to its existence; the other, by giving to every citizen the same opinions, the same passions, and the same interests."[21]

Madison and the Founders recognized that it was impossible to fully eliminate the problem. They created a system that would "frustrate faction," but they could not, since faction and fallibility are inherent in human nature, eliminate the dangers in a system that allows the people to have a free voice and freedom of conscience. They could only try to control the effects of faction, not the causes of it—fallible human nature and liberty. As Madison later stated in Federalist No. 51:

It may be a reflection on human nature, that such devices [checks and balances] should be necessary to control the abuses of government. But what is government itself, but the greatest of all reflections on human nature? If men were angels, no government would be necessary. If angels were to govern men, neither external nor internal controls on government would be necessary. In framing a government which is to be administered by men over men, the great difficulty lies in this: you must first enable the government to control the governed; and in the next place oblige it to control itself.[22]

The framers of the Constitution set about creating the first balanced republican form of government that obligated it to control itself. Not only did each branch have limited powers, but the federal government as a whole had limited powers, relegating powers to the states not enumerated in the Constitution. Empowering the states to govern themselves not only provided a "double security" for liberty,[23] but it was necessary to create a "more perfect Union" and "secure the Blessings of Liberty," as stated in the Preamble of the U.S. Constitution. Under federalism, the states are protected from federal overreach and afforded the privilege to pursue liberties and rule themselves as they see fit, given their relatively unique needs and values.

As mentioned earlier, the backstory of the U.S. Constitution also provides a revealing glimpse of the nature of wisdom. Learned delegates deeply versed in philosophy and history met from May 25 to September 17 in 1787 to discuss the challenges of creating a lasting republic that protected individual liberties, however imperfectly. John Adams provided a partial list of philosophers and philosophical historians whose thoughts informed the U.S. Constitution: Plato, Aristotle, Polybius, Cicero, Machiavelli, John Locke, Baron de Montesquieu, and David Hume.[24] The framers of the Constitution also had the benefit of learning from the failures of the Articles of Confederation, the first constitution of the United States, written in the fog of the Revolutionary War. The Articles, ratified in 1781, established a loose "league of friendships" among the thirteen states with an ineffectual, unicameral central government. The U.S. Constitutional Convention delegates not only relied on reason and revelation to craft the Constitution, but they also engaged in extended meaningful debate to revise and refine their thinking and writing. As iron sharpens iron (Proverbs 27:17) and examination exposes gaps in knowledge and understanding (Proverbs 18:17), the deliberative debates forged an unprecedented document and form of government.

The U.S. Constitution was the product of the delegates' depth of knowledge and understanding from their formal education and studies, evaluated life experiences under the Articles of Confederation, and dialectic discussions. The Supreme Court of the United States (SCOTUS) is an institution designed for the pursuit and practice of wisdom. It exists to render judgment, not to make or execute laws. The Justices are expected to be disposed to exercise judgment, not preferences.[25] The Justices are tasked to adjudicate some of the more complex dilemmas, those that indeed require wisdom. Their history and process reveal much about the nature of wisdom. One would think that nine of some of the brightest legal minds in the United States would agree 100 percent of the time on the interpretation and application of the laws regarding the same sets of facts. Yet according to the 2015 Supreme Court Compendium, the average percentage of unanimous and 5-4 decisions from 1970 to 2013 was 40.1 percent and 19.7 percent, respectively.[26] The differing judgments over the same sets of facts reveal that much of life is navigating complex dilemmas, having to adjudicate among competing cherished values.

Two separate but parallel 2003 U.S. Supreme Court decisions highlight the nature of wisdom as discerning distinctions and rendering decisions accordingly. Not only were the two decisions adjudicated in the same year, but both centered on affirmative action admission policies and shared the same Respondent, Lee Bollinger, president of the University of Michigan. What makes these two cases especially interesting is that the decisions appear contradictory. In *Grutter v. Bollinger*, the Court ruled in favor (5-4) of affirmative action in the law school's admission policy, while in *Gratz v. Bollinger*, the court ruled against (6-3) a race-conscious undergraduate admission policy.

At the risk of oversimplifying SCOTUS's long, complex, and controversial history with affirmative action policies, and for the exclusive purpose of illustrating the nature of dilemmas that SCOTUS confronts, suffice it to say that the two decisions confirmed that affirmative action admission policies are considered both appropriate and inappropriate, depending on the context. Jennifer Gratz and Barbara Grutter were both denied admission to their respective programs at the University of Michigan because of existing affirmative action policies. In *Gratz*, the court ruled that too much weight was awarded to race in the University's undergraduate admission policy, violating the Equal Protection Clause of the Fourteenth Amendment.[27] In *Grutter*, the court ruled that the school's attempt to foster diversity was compelling, and "unlike the program at issue in *Gratz v. Bollinger, ante*, the Law School awards no mechanical, predetermined diversity 'bonuses' based on race or ethnicity."[28] While there are winners and losers with every SCOTUS decision, that does not mean petitioners and respondents are proven right or wrong. It means that in each case, a particular value or set of values becomes first among equals, based upon each Justice's interpretation of the law, judicial temperament, legal and historical context, and legal precedent. But as evident by the split votes in each decision and the arguments presented, it boils down to making judgment calls based upon compelling values uniquely at work in different scenarios. These two cases are particularly interesting in that they deal with the same set of values but they yielded different outcomes.

Not all judgments coming from SCOTUS are wise, but the way SCOTUS adjudicates hedges its bets to make more wise judgments than unwise.[29] It is the Socratic process of rendering a decision that makes SCOTUS a wise institution. The process of rendering a decision begins with lawyers on both sides of the argument submitting a series of cogent briefs and counterarguments for the Justices to review prior to hearing oral arguments. The oral argument stage allows the Justices to ask probing and penetrating questions and gain deeper understanding and clarification of the issues at hand. Throughout the process, from start to finish, relevant case law is cited and used to inform the present decision. It is during what follows next, the Justices' Conference, that decisions are rendered, but only after each Justice has had the opportunity to state his or her view, ask questions, and/or raise concerns. Each Justice speaks without interruption, and every Justice speaks once before another Justice can speak twice. When all Justices are finished speaking, the call for the vote takes place and a final decision is rendered.[30]

The prolonged deliberative process of calm debate and disagreement deepens understanding and facilitates the emergence of wisdom, tapping into the more transcendent storyline(s) among the many other and equally compelling storylines at play in the given scenario. The SCOTUS written opinions reflect the process and often read like a ping-pong match, back and forth, as each argument is paired with the counterargument, concurring opinions with dissenting opinions, such that the reader gets a sense that the issue at hand received full consideration. That SCOTUS is diligent to establish why the winning opinion took preference over the other ones gives legitimacy to their decisions and models the nature of wisdom and how wisdom is acquired and practiced.[31]

The following story illustrates how the wisdom of a military commander averted bloodshed:

> During one of the many nineteenth-century riots in Paris the commander of an army detachment received orders to clear a city square by firing at the canaille (rabble). He commanded his soldiers to take up firing positions, their rifles leveled at the crowd; as a ghastly silence descended he drew his sword and shouted at the top of his lungs: "Mesdames, m'sieurs, I have orders to fire at the canaille. But as I see a great number of honest, respectable citizens before me, I request that they leave so that I can safely shoot the canaille." The square was empty in a few minutes.[32]

Fortunately, the commander had a sense of *sophia* that made him value life over following directions and preserving order. As a result, he shrewdly discerned a way to disperse the crowd as commanded. The commander demonstrated a wisdom found lacking in his superiors.

A poignant example of failure to recognize relevant storylines is recorded by Nikita Khrushchev, former premier of the Soviet Union (1953–1964), regarding the defection of Joseph Stalin's daughter Svetlanka.

> After complaining how wrong it had been for her to defect, Khrushchev suggests how the defection could have been possibly avoided with a different form of rhetoric. She did something stupid, but Svetlanka was dealt with stupidly, too—stupidly and rudely. Apparently, after her husband's funeral she went to our embassy in New Delhi. Benediktov was our ambassador there. I knew him. He's a very strait-laced person. Svetlanka said she wanted to stay in India for a few months, but Benediktov advised her to return immediately to the Soviet Union. This was stupid on his part. When a Soviet ambassador recommends that a citizen of the Soviet Union return home immediately, it makes the person suspicious. Svetlanka was particularly familiar with our habits in this regard. She knew it meant she wasn't trusted.
>
> What do I think should have been done? I'm convinced that if she had been treated differently, the regrettable episode would never have happened: When Svetlanka came to the embassy and said that she had to stay in India for two or three months, they should have told her, "Svetlanka Iosifovna, why only

three months? Get a visa for a year or two or even three years. You can get a visa and live here. Then, whenever you are ready, you can go back to the Soviet Union." If she had been given freedom of choice, her morale would have been boosted. They should have shown her that she was trusted. . . . And what if we had acted the way I think we should have and Svetlanka still hadn't returned home from India? Well, that would have been too bad but no worse than what happened.[33]

Another illustration of wisdom is the difference between good parenting and wise parenting. Parents get to nurture their progenies through nascency, infancy, childhood, adolescence, and adulthood. Good parents prepare their children for the next stage with a long-term goal of developing autonomous and good individuals who are prepared to navigate the vicissitudes of life. Good parents judiciously and diligently attend to their children's physical, emotional, cognitive, moral, psychological, social, and spiritual development. Wise parents do the same thing, but they do it differently. Good parents raise their children to be happy and make their beds for them ("I just want my child to be happy"), while wise parents raise their children to be responsible ("I want my child to take responsibility for his or her actions") and have their children make their own beds. Good parents teach their children right and wrong, while wise parents teach their children to discern what makes things right and wrong. Good parents want their children to have a happy life; wise parents want their children to have a meaningful life.

A life well-lived is evidence of wisdom when juxtaposed with lives not so well-lived, illustrating once again the nature of wisdom. A visit to an assisted living or nursing care facility provides visceral examples and contrasts between those who have lived wisely and those who have not lived so wisely. Some residents will have healthy dispositions and loving family members and friends at their side on a regular basis, while others have sick and dour dispositions with few visitors, if any. One author of this primer knew a multi-millionaire who died a lonely and unhappy man, estranged from his children and grandchildren and bitter toward many people in his life. It seemed that he learned only how to make a living and did not learn how to live wisely. That some lives are better lived than others is revealed in the different legacies people leave, not of financial wealth, but of the type and extent of influence and impact on others to live meaningful lives.

It is time to return to the nurse as the final example of wisdom for this primer. The nurse in the scenario provided at the opening of this chapter exercised both *sophia* and *phronesis* in her actions. She set up the IV as directed by the doctor. She called the doctor over to the patient and informed him that she had complied with his directive as far as her conscience would dictate. At that moment, she requested that the doctor be the one to initiate the IV. The nurse identified the relevant storylines at play in this scenario—honoring her convictions, the doctor's initial orders, and the patient's health. She found a solution that allowed her to honor the three major storylines at the same time by choosing to willfully disobey without disobeying by delegating the final decision back to the person in charge, demonstrating practical wisdom. It seemed that the nurse also understood that having the doctor look the patient in the eye prior to administering the IV would personalize the decision sufficiently for the doctor to reevaluate the certainty of his diagnosis, demonstrating more theoretical wisdom. In this scenario, the doctor actually took pause and decided upon another course of action, demonstrating wisdom on his part.

SUMMARY

Wisdom is the ability to identify multiple patterns and storylines in any given situation and triage beliefs, dispositions, and actions according to the more transcendent and noble truths so as to make the "right" things happen the "right" way. This still leaves some ambiguity, given what is "right" is based on what is true, perceived to be true, and the corresponding hierarchy of values. *Sophia* is more theoretical and discerns at the worldview level the content and ultimate *telos* for exercising *phronesis*. *Phronesis* is the practical application of *sophia* that discerns and pursues the appropriate balance among competing narratives, priorities, and values so as to optimize human flourishing at the individual and collective levels.

Wisdom is also enlightened judgment. But not all judgments are wise. The wise default to the more transcendent, veridical storylines while honoring the other storylines at the same time. For example, it is a good idea to speak the truth, wiser to speak the truth in love, and wisest to speak the truth in love with patience and instruction. When people fail to demonstrate wisdom, it is typically because they fail to discern competing narratives and values at work in any given situation.

Wisdom manifests itself in enlightened action. While wisdom is primarily an intellectual virtue, it is also a moral virtue. It cultivates and manifests itself in more elevated and noble thoughts, actions, and dispositions. For wisdom to be complete, it must accompany the other virtues. Wisdom is ultimately about human flourishing, the actual pursuing of the proper *teloses* or ends, not just the knowledge thereof. The endgame of wisdom is to be skilled at living; therefore, wisdom is ultimately a virtuous endeavor. The wise not only think about the right things, but they do them. To be wise is to be virtuous, and to be virtuous is to be wise.

For example, Aristotle and Confucius established that it takes wisdom to know when and how to be courageous (i.e., the Golden Mean), but can people be wise without courage? Why even worry about courage in the first place, unless one was disposed to have the right things happen the right way? If wisdom indicates that courage is necessary, not to act courageously would be inconsistent with wisdom. One could argue that there are cowardly and reckless wise people, just as there are courageous fools. Granted, wise people sometimes act cowardly or foolish, but it is the habits of virtue over time that manifest wisdom.

The description of the nature of wisdom provided above cannot but help be a bit incomplete, or at least not comprehensive enough to automatically capture the essence of wisdom because wisdom is so contextual. Each scenario, especially a consequential one, will have its own set of storylines and hierarchy of values. The wise person will be haunted with "What about this?" and "What about that?" when rendering judgments, and as a result, must be able to tolerate levels of ambiguity associated with parallel and/or competing truths.

Knowing the nature of wisdom is a starting point to understanding wisdom. What follows are a few basic principles to acquire, practice, and teach wisdom, or, at least, to predispose people toward it.

ACQUIRING WISDOM

The nature of wisdom reveals that before people can judiciously navigate the multiple patterns and storylines at play in life, they must first be able to identify them. This is accomplished by gaining both a broad and deep knowledge and understanding of the truth about how and why life works as it does and the conditions that promote human flourishing. Growing in knowledge and understanding are cognitive and experiential endeavors. People need to animate their inner philosopher, theologian, psychologist, sociologist, economist, biologist, artist, musician, writer, and scholar to identify and develop holistic insights of the world and, by doing so, enlarge their personal experiences.

The wisdom of Abraham Lincoln and many other successful leaders was due in large part to their insatiable appetite for reading and learning.[34] Unfortunately, far too many people are taught and/or are content to acquire knowledge without understanding. People may know what they believe, but unfortunately many do not know why they know and believe what they know and believe. Acquiring wisdom requires ever-expanding levels of knowledge and understanding of life and truth. Axiomatically, acquiring wisdom requires people to be formal and informal lifelong learners who read and study reflectively both broadly and deeply.

As people mature, they acquire additional knowledge and levels of understanding along the way, yet not all people will acquire wisdom as they age. How is it then that far too many people do not become wiser as they get older? Why is there a low correlation between age and wisdom? Experience is necessary, but not sufficient. Critical evaluation of beliefs and life experiences are additional co-requisites to wisdom. Wisdom does not automatically come from experience and its correlate age. Wisdom comes with experience and age only when such experiences are evaluated. This is the wisdom of Socrates's axiom—an unexamined life is not worth living.

Highly skilled athletes and performers are formed in the crucible of intensive, feedback-rich practices and rehearsals. Far too many people go through life having a plethora of experiences but stop short of growing in wisdom because they fail to fully evaluate and apply lessons that make for new learning and insights. To become skilled at life requires consistent feedback-rich learning. It is through reflection and evaluation that people learn and grow from experience. In this regard, wisdom is a performance that consists of many dress rehearsals and practices in which the director provides constructive feedback until the respective parts are mastered. Acquiring wisdom requires people to be their best critic—seeking from others and providing themselves with ongoing, candid, and aspirational evaluations, tempered with grace. This can be done without brooding introspection, but rather along the line of what the French call *l'esprit de l'escalier*, the spirit of the staircase. It refers to the things people wish they would have said or done differently on their way out.

Virtue is not only a means and manifestation of wisdom; it is a tutor to wisdom. The wise become wiser when they gain additional understandings about the nature of reality through certain practices. For example, exercising temperance, courage, and fortitude yields nuanced insights and understandings of how life best works. People learn what is good by being good. Morally good people increase their chances of acquiring wisdom, because as they practice virtue, they gain experiential understandings of what is true, good, and beautiful. The implementation of these understandings promotes human flourishing. People grow in wisdom by practicing virtue.

Humility is a virtue worthy of special mention in relation to wisdom. Wise people rightly understand that they are not omniscient, omnipresent, and perfect. As a result, they recognize that knowledge and understanding are bounded. Humility is "the golden mean between hubris and timidity and between haughtiness and inferiority."[35] Arrogance and superiority preclude people from seeking wisdom, while timidity and inferiority make wisdom seem out of reach.

Wisdom is about navigating moral and ethical dilemmas, and it requires people to acquire a certain level of moral reasoning and development. Most people would say that it is wrong to steal. But when asked what makes stealing wrong, the answers will vary. The research on moral development revealed that children will respond differently than adolescents, who may or may not respond differently than adults, depending on their level of moral reasoning. Lawrence Kohlberg's empirical theory of moral development shaped subsequent research on the nature of moral judgment.[36] While Kohlberg's seminal theory has been nuanced, its basic features remain and demonstrate that people employ different justifications when rendering moral judgments, depending on their age and experiences. Kohlberg identified three levels of moral reasoning, each with two stages: preconventional (egocentric); conventional (sociocentric); and postconventional (principle-centric).

When children (five to ten years of age) are asked the equivalent of why it is wrong to steal a candy bar, the typical response is because they don't want to get into trouble. When asked why they should do good and behave, the typical response is to get a reward. For example, children are often told that they must eat their vegetables in order to get dessert (reward). The justifications in the preconventional stage are egocentric in that they are based on what is in it for the child when making a moral choice.

Typical adolescents (ten to sixteen years of age) will probably say that it is wrong to steal a candy bar because the act will disappoint their parents and it is against the law. The reasoning becomes more sociocentric because it involves what others will think. Older children behave to please their parents and teachers and avoid misbehavior so as to not disappoint those whose opinions of them matter. This does not mean they are still not egocentric in their moral judgments at times, but that as they mature, they appreciate and recognize that social norms become more significant when making moral decisions.

The third level of moral judgment that Kohlberg identified is principle-centered reasoning. When adults are asked why it is wrong to steal a candy bar, hopefully they identify that what ultimately makes stealing wrong, even a candy bar, is that it dishonors the respective proprietors by robbing them of the fruit of their labor and the rightful ownership of the goods in question. Honoring people and their right to private ownership by not stealing is not only a valid social contract (i.e., principles of cooperation and reciprocity necessary for society to function), but a matter of respect and appreciation for proprietors' work and livelihood. Principle-centered thinking appeals to higher-level reasoning that ultimately justifies why moral acts are worthy of punishment/reward and/or are disappointing/pleasing to others.

Principled-level thinking is necessary since most of life is navigating dilemmas with multiple good options rather than solving problems with one absolute right or wrong answer. Dilemmas arise when cherished values are in conflict and involve choices among two or more rights. Rushworth Kidder identified in his book, *How Good People Make Tough Choices: Resolving the Dilemma of Ethical Living*, the four most common right-versus-right dilemmas: Mercy versus Justice; Short Term versus Long Term; Truth versus Loyalty; and Individual versus Community.[37] Principled-level reasoning is also called ethical situationalism, not to be confused with situational ethics. Ethical situationalism holds that "objective moral principles are to be applied differently in different contexts, whereas ethical relativism denies universal ethical principles altogether."[38] SCOTUS Justices engage in principled-centered exchanges when they argue the various sides of the law to adjudicate what values are *primus inter pares*—first among equals in a particular situation.

The disheartening news is that most adults do not make it to the third level of moral reasoning identified by Kohlberg.[39] It is a sad commentary when adults are not able to articulate what makes something wrong beyond, "I will get in trouble" or "it is against the law," and are unable to answer what makes something so wrong that it will get them in trouble for it or that a law had to be made in the first place. Society is good at instilling values and virtues by emphasizing what is right and wrong but fails when it does not teach *why* things are right and wrong. A simple remedy to cultivate higher levels of moral and ethical reasoning, a precursor to wisdom, is to coach children to evaluate what makes certain behaviors wrong or correct and nudge them to the next level of moral reasoning in prime teaching moments.

Acquiring the ability to triage multiple storylines and make discerning judgments requires people to be curious lifelong learners, be periodically introspective, develop virtuous habits, and engage in higher levels of moral reasoning. While there are other pre- and co-requisites to acquire wisdom, these four habits are foundational and catalytic to other important mindsets and habits conducive to understanding and acquiring wisdom.

PRACTICING WISDOM

As an intellectual virtue, wisdom is a nuanced understanding of the nature and patterns of reality that discerns the storylines that promote human flourishing. As a moral virtue, wisdom is the pursuit of behaviors that best promote human flourishing, aligning thoughts, feelings, and behaviors with the more transcendent and noble storylines. Acquiring wisdom is a feedback-intensive developmental journey. While it is acquired over time in concert with specific habits, it is also practiced and lived in the moment.

Wisdom is an iterative and cumulative practice; wisdom begets wisdom, which begets more wisdom. Wise adults tend to be wiser than wise youth, though wise youth tend to be wiser than foolish elders. Sternberg described this as people having depths of wisdom, ranging from shallow to deep.[40] The best way to practice wisdom is to choose to be wise. When confronted with how and what to think and act and what habits to cultivate, people should consistently ask, "What would wisdom do?" Better yet, "What would *sophia* and *phronesis* dictate?" These questions would force people to reevaluate taken-for-granted thoughts and habits and prioritize their values and virtues. These questions would help people keep multiple storylines and the ultimate set of whys at the forefront of their thinking and actions (*sophia*) and make corresponding choices based upon the situational contexts of the respective decisions (*phronesis*).

People with limited knowledge and understanding, fewer life experiences, less maturity in the virtues, and in the early stages of moral reasoning can still be wise for their age, even though they might not be as wise as people a bit more seasoned in life. By asking, "What wisdom would do?" regardless of age, inquirers are forced to identify options and evaluate ultimately what make some options better than others. As a result, they seek counsel from others, as there is wisdom in the counsel of many (Proverbs 11:14; 15:22), but prior to seeking counsel, they would evaluate whom to ask for counsel, recognizing that some counselors are better than others (Psalm 1). By asking, "What would wisdom do?" choices like what kind of friends to choose, whom to date, what to study in college, what to buy, whom to hire or fire, and whom to vote for take on new import.

Discerning the right and best of the available thoughts and actions is the first step in practicing wisdom. The necessary next step is to act accordingly. If *sophia* reveals that certain types of friends are more beneficial than others and *phronesis* identifies who and how to secure those friends, it then follows that wisdom is complete only when certain types of friendships are established. People can demonstrate the intellectual virtue of wisdom without its moral component, evidenced by "do what I say, not what I do," but it falls short in achieving the higher ends.

A third step, axiomatic to the first two, is to reevaluate beliefs and choices in light of new learning acquired by new acts of wisdom. In this regard, practicing wisdom is the same as acquiring wisdom through healthy reflection and introspection. Choosing to grow in understanding and wisdom is itself an act of wisdom.

TEACHING WISDOM

Wisdom by nature is didactic. To have wisdom is to teach wisdom. The love and fruit of wisdom compels people to pass it on to others and future generations. Parents, teachers, bosses, and leaders can create conditions conducive for the teaching of wisdom. They can structure wisdom learning opportunities for those under their tutelage and mentorship. The few practices suggested below show that it can be done with relative ease.

It seems teaching for wisdom begins at home with parents not only teaching right and wrong, but also teaching what makes particular attitudes and actions right and wrong. Parents can also expose their children to proverbs and have them read, for example, *Aesop's Fables*, William Bennett's *The Children's Book of Virtues*, and Mortimer Adler and Charles Van Doren's *How to Read a Book: The Classic Guide to Intelligent Reading*.[41] Parents can assign reading homework to their children, exposing them to a variety of topics and thoughts. As children begin school, parents can emphasize understanding over knowledge. This is as simple as occasionally asking their children why different classes and even class assignments ultimately matter. It is common for parents to tell their children to finish high school so that they can go to college so that they can get a good job. Securing a good job is important, but what do they do with their life once they secure a good job? What is the use of a good job if they have not learned how to live life well? Finally, parents can orchestrate the type of friends their children spend time with. Parents should strategically vet whom their children associate with, knowing that bad company can corrupt good morals (1 Cor. 15:33) and that good company tends to promote good morals. Assessing who is bad company does not excuse the wise from exercising empathy and including others, but it does require them to exercise degrees of engagement.

Teachers—society, for that matter—can alter the aims of education to be more than the transfer of knowledge. Adler's *The Paideia Proposal: An Educational Manifesto*, Sternberg's *Teaching for Wisdom, Intelligence, Creativity and Success*, and Maxwell's *From Knowledge to Wisdom: A Revolution for Science and the Humanities* document that it can and must be done.[42] They provide insights and principles for teachers to coach students to higher levels of thinking and understanding through Socratic dialogues and seminar discussions in each subject area. They advocate the study of core knowledge, great literature and biographies (of lives well-lived), and reflective engagement in the fine arts. Deciding what knowledge is of most worth is the perennial task of every teacher, principal, and school board member, one without readily agreeable answers, yet when the aim is cultivating wisdom, the curriculum takes a different pattern. A starting point would require students to periodically evaluate why they are learning what they are learning—evaluating how their subjects relate, what they reveal about the nature of reality, and the implications for living a good life. That simple practice, albeit not necessarily easy, can have a butterfly effect on education.

What CEO, executive, manager, or supervisor does not want their employees to practice wisdom in the workplace? Conducting periodic after-action reviews and ethical forums allows teams to learn from each other, grow from mistakes, and navigate ethical dilemmas. Facilitating opportunities for people to craft and share jobs expands their understanding of the organization and relational networks beyond what they experience in their work silos. Providing in-house educational opportunities in diverse realms of learning that cultivate deeper understanding and aesthetics for life makes for better-engaged and higher-performing employees. It may sound quixotic to periodically pay employees to engage in learning outside of their specific job duties, but such intentionality can have an intangible impact on the bottom lines found in every collective.

At minimum, parents, teachers, and employers can create inquisitive home, school, and work environments, respectively, to teach for wisdom. Inquisitiveness can be characterized as the "question-asking virtue," and "inquisitiveness plays a distinctive role in both the initiation of intellectually virtuous inquiry and in the cultivation of intellectually virtuous character. It is a primary intellectual virtue to educate for."[43] Unfortunately, that natural curiosity that preschool children are known for actually diminishes with age, coincidently at the time they enter school.[44] The "walking question marks" focus on conforming once they enter society's formal organizations, only to lose their inquisitive spirit to the detriment of acquiring wisdom.

CONCLUSION

Wisdom understands the patterns at work in the universe (i.e., multiple storylines), discerns the more transcendent and noble patterns to pursue in particular situations, and aligns beliefs, dispositions, and habits with those patterns that best promote human flourishing. It is an intellectual virtue born out of enlightened knowledge and an understanding of truth and universal patterns. It is necessarily a moral virtue for the appropriate *teloses* to be realized. Intellectual wisdom without the companion virtues defaults to punditry. The other virtues without wisdom risk being reckless and meaningless.

Wisdom begins with a quest for truth that involves the ongoing careful and deliberative discernment over why particular beliefs, dispositions, and actions should take precedence over others. Wisdom understands truth in relation to other truths. It is greater than just knowing and understanding more things; it is knowing and understanding what makes beliefs, dispositions, and habits worthier and more meaningful than others. The fruit of wisdom is human flourishing. It equips people to be especially skilled at navigating life successfully in a world filled with challenges and dilemmas and thrive in their personal and professional endeavors.

There is an amazing level of congruence of thought on the nature of wisdom found in the philosophical, theological, and empirical traditions, specifically:

1. Wisdom is attainable, albeit not easily. This requires people to be lovers of wisdom who diligently seek to understand, acquire, practice, and teach wisdom.
2. Wisdom discerns ultimate ends (*teloses*) and the proper means to make "right things" happen the "right way." It is a telocentric way of thinking about and conducting life based upon people's common and unique features and purposes.
3. Wisdom promotes human flourishing. It discerns and cultivates the better thoughts, dispositions, and habits that help individuals and the collective thrive.
4. Wisdom assumes that Truth and truth exist and are discernable, albeit at times hidden. This encumbers people to be lovers of truth

who consistently evaluate their metaphysical, epistemological, and axiological assumptions and conclusions.

5. Wisdom is predicated on depths of knowledge and understanding. One cannot be skilled at living without a nuanced understanding of life, of both the universals and the particulars, and one cannot achieve understanding without a foundational knowledge of the nature and meaning of life. At the same time, it is possible to have knowledge and understanding and fail to exercise wisdom.

6. Wisdom is developmental. It not only takes time to grow in knowledge, understanding, and wisdom, but it also takes time to experience the cognitive, emotional, psychosocial, and spiritual stages of growth. At the same time, advancing in age does not guarantee wisdom.

7. Wisdom is contextual. What might be wise in one set of circumstances will not necessarily be wise in another context because of the situational variables. However, the process of discernment and the nature of wisdom are the same regardless of the scenario.

8. Wisdom is an intellectual virtue. It is the ability to discern multiple perspectives or storylines at any one point in time and align one's beliefs, choices, and habits into the more transcendent and noble ones. Wisdom is a form of perspective-taking of and within overlapping systems.

9. Wisdom is a moral virtue. It seeks the good and does good. Virtuous character is concurrent to wisdom since wisdom involves understanding and doing what is right and good. At the same time, one can be good and do what is right without being wise, and one can be wise and experience moral and ethical lapses.

10. Wisdom involves both *sophia* and *phronesis*. *Sophia* deals with ultimate values and truth. As a result, *sophia* is more philosophical and theological. *Phronesis* deals with the application of values and truth in real life. Thus, it is more practical and informed by *sophia*.

Wisdom is necessary if people are to be especially skilled at living, equipped to thrive in their individual and collective journeys. The good news is that wisdom is readily accessible to those who seek it. While the path to wisdom is the more arduous one, and, as a result, the path less traveled, those who do take the time to understand, acquire, practice, and teach wisdom will have the advantageous perspectives necessary to pursue the good life and promote human flourishing.

REFLECTION AND DISCUSSION QUESTIONS

1. What is the nature of truth and its relationship to wisdom?
2. How do people know if their conclusions about the nature of reality are true?
3. How are *sophia* and *phronesis* two sides to the same coin?
4. What does the definition of wisdom provided in this chapter suggest about the nature of wisdom?
5. Why and how is wisdom an intellectual and moral virtue?
6. How can people acquire wisdom?
7. How and why is virtue both a manifestation of wisdom and a tutor for wisdom?
8. How can people practice wisdom?
9. How can people teach wisdom?
10. How will you live and lead differently as the result of a better understanding of the nature of wisdom?

NOTES

PREFACE

1. Plato, *Phaedrus*, 15.278c-d.

CHAPTER 1

1. Russell, 1912/2001, 91.
2. Ibid., 94.
3. Werther & Werther, 2015.
4. Reiss, 1982, 156 and 164.
5. Russell, 1912/2001, 409.
6. Boethius, ca. 524/2002, Book I. Sections in the *Consolations of Philosophy* are separated by books, the equivalent of chapters.
7. Job and Ecclesiastes are Wisdom Books in the Bible and are described in chapter 2. Seneca (c. 4 B.C.E.–C.E. 65) was a Roman moral philosopher.
8. Zeno was a Greek philosopher and an elderly contemporary of Socrates.
9. Boethius, Book I.
10. Ibid., Book II.
11. Ibid., Book IV.
12. Ibid.
13. Reiss, 1982, 130.
14. Boethius, Book V.

15. Xenophon was a philosopher and historian. Aristophanes was a Greek comedic playwright. Both were contemporaries of Plato.

16. Russell, 1946/2004, 137.

17. Plato, ca. 360 B.C.E.

18. For Plato, the three classes of society mirror the three parts of the human soul: appetitive—human pleasures and basic needs (producers); spirited—human need for respect and esteem (auxiliaries); and rational—pursuit of truth, knowing, and beauty (guardians).

19. Plato, *Republic*, Books II–IV.

20. *Appetites* refers to the seat of human desires and pleasures, often referred to by Plato as "money-loving," given that money is required to satisfy the various human lusts.

21. Plato provided his famous Allegory of the Cave to illustrate how people see shadows of the true Forms. As a result, perceptions of reality based upon the senses are incomplete, if not misleading. For Plato, knowledge of the true Forms is obtained through philosophical reasoning.

22. Plato, *Republic*, 488d–489a.

23. Plato, ca. 360 B.C.E.

24. Taylor, 2012, 463.

25. The *Republic* focused on an ideal city, Callipolis (the beautiful city), a sort of utopia. The City of the Magnetes as referred to in the *Laws* was, in contrast, considered an "attainable" city, within which idealism is tempered by realistic and practical considerations.

26. Plato and Aristotle used the word *eudaimonia* for happiness based upon fulfillment that facilitates flourishing, in contrast to the contemporary meaning, which views happiness as a feeling, often based upon circumstances. The writers of the Declaration of Independence had the former definition of *eudaimonia* in mind when they included the construct of happiness in the document.

27. Laws are treated as necessities to promote desired values for individuals to thrive in their collectives.

28. Plato, *Laws*, 631.

29. Plato, *Laws*, Book II.

30. Book X takes a diversion to address philosophical and theological assumptions about the essence, definitions, and names of the divine, soul, and impiety.

31. Aristotle, *Politics*, 4.1288^{b}1.

32. Aristotle, ca. 350 B.C.E

33. Aristotle's *NE* is to his *Politics* as Plato's *Republic* is to the *Laws*. The former of each consists of treatises on how and why to live virtuously, according to a univer-

sal moral purpose, while the latter provides perspectives on how to live wisely in the context of the polis, or larger community.

34. Aristotle wrote two different books on ethics, *Nicomachean Ethics* (*NE*) and *Eudemian Ethics* (*EE*), appellations referencing early editors of the respective works. The reference to "the ethical" in *Politics* can be to *NE* or *EE*, and since both books have much in common, a case could be made for either book.

35. Aristotle, *Politics*, 4.1295ª11.

36. Aristotle noted in his *Politics* that virtue and wisdom are necessary for happiness. He explicitly stated, "Let us acknowledge then that each one has just so much happiness as he has of virtue and wisdom, and of virtuous and wise action. God is a witness to us of this truth, for he is happy and blessed, not by reason of any external good, but in himself and by reason of his own nature" (Book VII).

37. Aristotle, *Nicomachean Ethics*, 1.1.1094a2-3.

38. Ibid., 2.3.1104a24-26.

39. Ibid., Book VI.

40. Ibid., 7.1141b22-24.

41. Ibid., 6.13.1145a.1-2.

42. Aristotle, *The Art of Rhetoric*, ca. 350 B.C.E., Book II.

43. Aristotle, *Nicomachean Ethics*, 8.1.1155a5-6; 8.1.1155a23.

44. Ibid., 8.3.1156b7-9.

45. Ibid., 8.3.1156b25-26.

46. How to use a cutting knife well is an art, or *techne*.

47. A professor of Chinese history and philosophy at Harvard University, Tu Wei-Ming has written numerous books on Confucian learning, humanism, and philosophy, including *Neo-Confucian Thought in Action* (1976); *Humanity and Self-Cultivation: Essays in Confucian Thought* (1980); and *The Way, Learning and Politics: Perspectives on the Confucian Intellectual* (1988).

48. Martin, 1998, 4.

49. Slingerland, 2003, vii.

50. Ibid., vii.

51. Leys, 1997, xvi.

52. Martin, 1998, 4.

53. Slingerland, 2003, 6. The primer relies on Slingerland's (2003) translation of the *Analects* for its extensive commentary of the language and texts. He provided a rich context not found in other translations, such that without such context the uninitiated would miss out on subtleties of the text. The selected commentaries of the different passages also "give a sense of the variety of commentarial tradition, as well as the sorts of debates that it is engendered" (xv), revealing a range of acceptable interpretations that treat the text as a whole grounded in its historical context. The

capitalization of "the Way," and other words to follow, are Slingerland's way of alerting the reader to a distinct and key construct in Confucius philosophy.

54. Ibid.

55. Ni (2017) noted that the word *zhi* in the Analects "covers a range of meanings, including 'knowledge,' 'to know,' 'understand,' 'realize,' 'recognize,' 'comprehend,' and it is used also for homophonous extension, *zhi* 'wisdom' or 'being wise'" (72).

56. Slingerland, 2003, 238.

57. Connolly, 2013, 270–71.

58. Ibid., 283.

59. Slingerland, 2003, 98.

60. Slingerland (2003) noted that the *Analects* is a "somewhat heterogenous collection of material from different time periods" (xiv), known as strata. Slingerland concluded, "Though no doubt representing different time periods and somewhat different concerns, the various strata of the Analects display enough consistency in terminological use, conceptual repertoire, and general religious viewpoint to allow us to treat the text as a whole" (109).

61. Slingerland, 2003, 241.

62. Yu, 2006, 335.

63. Ibid., 341.

64. Slingerland, 2003, 243.

65. Renima, Tiliouine, and Estes, 2016.

66. Mohammed, 2012, 2–3.

67. Elayyan, 2014.

68. Renima, Tiliouine, and Estes, 2016.

69. Rubenstein, 2003.

70. Gutas, "Al-Farabi," 2010, 20.

71. Black, 2002, 110.

72. Fakhry, 2004, 114.

73. Goodman, 1992.

74. Renima, Tiliouine, and Estes, 2016, 41.

75. Gutas, "Avicenna," 2010, 112 and 114.

76. Burrell, 2002, 198 and 196.

77. Akasoy, 2010, 111.

78. Fakhry, 2004, 282.

79. Renima, Tiliouine, and Estes, 2016, 42.

80. Pasnau, 2011, 34.

81. Ibid., 38.

82. Taylor, 2002, 193–94.

83. De Mowbray, 2004, 1. While *handmaiden* is a term laden with negative overtones, "the original and principal meaning of the concept of philosophy as a servant of theology was that philosophy had a part to play in the development of rational Christianity and that it was mainly used to combat those who wished to reject all secular knowledge" (De Mowbray, 2004, 2). Moreland (2020) noted that theology tends to get sloppy without the aid of philosophy and demonstrated how philosophy can lead to more robust theology.

84. Plato, *Apology*, 38a5-6.

CHAPTER 2

1. Ogden, 1978, 14.
2. Worthing, 1994, 403.
3. Ibid.
4. The New Testament is part of the Bible and consists of twenty-seven books on the life and teachings of Jesus Christ and the essential tenets of Christianity.
5. Morgan, 2010, 42 and 49.
6. *TaNaK* is an acronym for the canon of the Hebrew Bible. The Torah includes the first five books and is referred to as the Law. The Nevi'im includes the prophets, and the Ketuvi'im includes the writings.
7. Wisdom is personified as a woman in Proverbs and is the reason Boethius treated philosophy as a lady.
8. It is important to note that while each major religious text advocates for the quest for wisdom, each text also provides a different "wisdom" because of different assumptions and messages about the nature of God. Since the four religious traditions cited offer differing—and in some cases, antithetical—views about God, the seeker of wisdom probes not only the respective claims, but also the veracity of such claims. In this regard, wisdom involves both the pursuit and acquisition of truth. The search for wisdom is ultimately a quest for truth (i.e., the nature of reality) so that one can align his or her beliefs and actions to live congruently with truth.
9. There are other books devoted to evaluating which faith tradition best aligns with reality, such as Geisler and Watkins's (2003) *Worlds Apart*, Keller's (2008) *The Reason for God: Belief in an Age of Skepticism*, and Poplin's (2014) *Is Reality Secular: Testing the Assumptions of Four Global Worldviews*.
10. Bartholomew and O'Dowd, 2011.
11. The detailed accounting of the tribes of Israel is a testimony to God's faithfulness. The author's documentation, by name, of Abraham's descendants is provided as evidence of God's faithfulness to his promise recorded in Genesis 12.

12. Willmington, 2009, 1.

13. A key to interpreting Ecclesiastes correctly is to understand the use of the phrase "under the sun." Solomon used the phrase twenty-nine times in the book as a literary device to signal the reader that comments to follow are based upon the premise that God was not in the equation. This is in contrast to other sections in his didactic autobiography where he draws other conclusions when God is in the equation.

14. What is known as the *protoevangelium*. Dr. Sailhamer observed that the Jewish reader, upon reading Genesis 3:15, would have a visceral response of awe and anticipation, knowing something big was being announced that automatically begged the question—who will this be? Ever since, the Jewish community has been looking for the promised Messiah.

15. The Sermon has structural and content parallels to the wisdom literature of the Hebrew Bible and the book of James.

16. Carson, 1984, 130.

17. Ansary, 2009.

18. Ali, 2002.

19. Hermeneutics is the science and art of the interpretation of written and verbal communication.

20. The five pillars are: 1. Testimony of faith; 2. Prayer; 3. Charity; 4. Fasting; and 5. Pilgrimage.

21. Ansary, 2009, 9.

22. The first number cites the chapter, or surah, and the second number cites the verse within the surah in the Quran.

23. Ali, 2002, 262.

24. *Islam* is Arabic for "submission."

25. Ali, 2002, 533.

26. Ibid., 1.

27. After Mohammad's death, the scribes of the Quran wanted to make sure they retained the actual words of Allah as reported by Mohammad before the sayings were lost. This, in part, explains the reason for nonthematic or chronological ordering of the surahs.

28. Khalidi, 2009, xii.

29. Flood, 2009; Leach, 2014; Smith, 1992.

30. Chaudhuri et al., 2003; Dhavamony, 1982. The Rgveda consists of more than one thousand hymns to a pantheon of gods. The Samaveda is almost entirely verses from the Rgveda. The Yajurveda is a collection of ritual and ceremonial practices. The Atharvaveda consists of hymns, spells, and incantations and is considered by some as inferior and not on par with the other three Vedas (Leach, 2014; Young, 2010).

31. Leach, 2014, 18.
32. Chaudhuri et al., 2003; Dhavamony, 1982; Young, 2010.
33. Chaudhuri et al., 2003; Dhavamony, 1982.
34. Dhavamony, 1982, 5.
35. Chaudhuri et al., 2003; Dhavamony, 1982.
36. Hume, 1931, 2.
37. Ibid., vii.
38. Ibid., 9.
39. Ibid., vii.
40. The name indicates the title of the Upanishad being referenced. The subsequent numbers indicate the section and line number of the verse being cited. If the particular Upanishad has only one section, the second number represents the line number being cited.
41. The Bhagavad Gita is part of the Ramayana Epic and the Mahabharata Epic.
42. Hume, 1931.
43. Meditation in Hinduism involves reflective chanting and silence so as to free one's mind from counterproductive thoughts and distractions and enter a state of nothingness so that one can experience the Atman. In contrast, meditation in the Bible involves a deep reflection on biblical texts with a fully engaged mind to ascertain correct interpretations and applications of the content. The latter focuses on filling the mind, while the former is about emptying the mind.
44. Hume (1931) states that "this is Yoga (from the root yuj, meaning to 'join,' 'yoke,' 'harness'), a harnessing of the senses and mind from the falsely manifold objects and thoughts, and at the same time a union with the unitary blissful Self" (68).
45. Agoramoorthy, 2014, 558. "Guru is a Sanskrit word with the syllables Gu meaning 'darkness' or 'ignorance' and Ru meaning 'light or dispeller.' . . . It is therefore held in high respect as the divine light that dispels the darkness of ignorance."
46. Jeste and Vahia, 2008.
47. Lord Krishna is the Supreme Being in the Gita, while Brahman is the supreme existence in the Upanishads.
48. *Enstasy* (Greek, *en-stasis*, "standing into") is the reflexive flow of consciousness or state of mind free from physical and mental experiences (i.e., experiencing nothing) so as to be free to experience peace and harmony of mind, body, and soul. Enstasy is achieved through Hindu meditation and yoga.
49. Jeste and Vahia, 2008, 203.

CHAPTER 3

1. Lennox, 2009, 29.
2. Erikson, 1985.
3. Erikson, 1964, 133.
4. Clayton and Birren, 1980.
5. Holliday and Chandler, 1986.
6. Sternberg, 1990, 144.
7. Ibid., 155.
8. Ibid., 155–56.
9. Ardelt, 2003, 282.
10. Ibid., 277.
11. Ibid., 278.
12. Ibid.
13. Ibid., 279.
14. Ibid.
15. Ibid., 279–80.
16. Baltes, Glück, and Kunzmann, 2002, 329.
17. Ibid., 327.
18. Ibid., 331.
19. Staudinger, 2013, 8.
20. Baltes, Glück, and Kunzmann, 2002.
21. Ibid., 337.
22. Ibid.
23. Balts, Glück, and Kunzmann, 2002; Baltes and Staudinger, 2000; Staudinger, 2013.
24. Sternberg (2013) highlighted the distinction between general and personal wisdom by listing leaders considered wise in their service to the public, but plagued by their own vices and infidelities.
25. Staudinger, 2013, 10.
26. Sternberg, "Still Searching," 2015.
27. Sternberg, 2007, 108.
28. Ibid.
29. Sternberg, "Still Searching," 2015, 109.
30. Ibid.
31. Ibid.
32. Sternberg, 2007.
33. Ibid., 152.
34. Sternberg, 2013, 59 and 62.

35. Sternberg, 2004, 164.
36. Ibid., 164–65.
37. Sternberg, 2003; Dweck, 2007.
38. Sternberg, 2003, 235.
39. Dweck, 2007.
40. Kaufman and Sternberg, 2010, xiii.
41. Joyce, Weil, and Showers, 1992, 220.
42. Ericsson et al., 2006.
43. Sternberg, 2003, 188.
44. Ericsson et al., 2006; Kaufman and Sternberg, 2010.
45. Peterson and Seligman, 2004, 12.
46. Peterson and Seligman, 2004.
47. Ibid., 3.
48. Ibid., 4.
49. Ibid., 5.
50. Ibid., 13–14.
51. Donald Clifton and Markus Buckingham are pioneers in strength-based assessments and coauthors of *Now, Discover Your Strengths*. Mihaly Csikszentmihalyi is a leading researcher in the field of positive psychology and the author of *Flow: The Psychology of Optimal Experience*.
52. Howard Gardner is the Hobbs research professor of cognition and education with the Harvard Graduate School of Education and author of *Multiple Intelligences: New Horizons*.
53. Peterson and Seligman, 2004, 15.
54. Ibid., 35.
55. Ibid., 39.
56. Ibid.
57. Peterson and Seligman, 2004, 627.
58. Sternberg et al., 2006, 323.
59. Glück et al., 2013, 1.
60. Barabási and Bonabeau, 2003.
61. Bak, 1997; Buchanan, 2001.
62. Koch, 1998, 13.
63. Ibid.
64. Shoup and Studer, 2010, 21.
65. Stokes and Iversen, 1962; Zingher, 2014.
66. Shoup and Studer, 2010, 13.
67. Ibid., 17–18.
68. Ohno, 1988, 17.

69. Ibid., 17.

CHAPTER 4

1. Most controversial debates on the nature of truth happen when people treat truth with a small *t* the same as truth with a big *T* and/or fail to distinguish the difference between metaphysics (what is Truth and truth) and epistemology (how we know Truth and truth).
2. John Godfrey Saxe, 1873.
3. Keeney, 1983; Kuhn, 1996; and Osborne, 1997.
4. Geisler and Watkins, 2003.
5. Kuhn, 1996.
6. Moreland and Craig, 2003, 13.
7. Anacker and Shoup, 2014.
8. Chung-Ming and Woodman, 1995, 538.
9. Plato, *Apology*, 38a.
10. Schwartz and Sharpe, 2010, 23. Relying on Aristotle, they documented what they call the "wisdom deficit" and how "detailed rules and procedures, however well intentioned, are undermining the skill that wisdom requires" and "incentives, however well meaning, are undermining the will that wisdom requires."
11. Ibid., 17.
12. Ibid., 18.
13. Franklin, 1839, 84.
14. Three delegates present that day chose not to sign given they were not fully satisfied with the final iteration.
15. Owens, 2015.
16. Paulsen and Paulsen, 2015, 24.
17. Grey, 1984.
18. Lincoln, 1863.
19. That the Constitution can be cited allows readers to start "on the same page" and demonstrates the wisdom of a written Constitution.
20. Paulsen and Paulsen, 2015, 35.
21. Madison, Federalist No. 10, 72–73.
22. Madison, Federalist No. 51, 319.
23. Madison, Federalist No. 51, 320.
24. Reck, 1985.
25. Hamilton, Federalist No. 78.

26. Epstein et al., 2015. The average percent of unanimous and 5-4 decisions from 1900 to 1969 was 50.9 percent and 6.7 percent, respectively.
27. *Gratz v. Bollinger*, 539 U.S. 244, 2003.
28. *Grutter v. Bollinger*, 539 U.S. 306, 337, 2003.
29. This process is not infallible. SCOTUS has overturned previous rulings in spite of *stare decisis*—Latin for "to stand by things decided"—relying on precedent. The fact that it is fewer than 2 percent suggests that the process affords SCOTUS the conditions for rendering wise judgments (Shendruk, 2018).
30. Supreme Court Procedures, United States Courts, 2020.
31. John Stuart Mill (1859/2003) captured the essence of understanding and wisdom when he noted that "he who knows only his own side of the case, knows little of that. His reasons may be good, and no one may have been able to refute them. But if he is equally unable to refute the reasons on the opposite side; if he does not so much as know what they are, he has no ground for preferring either opinion" (104).
32. Watzlawick, Weakland, and Fisch, 1974, 81.
33. Khrushchev, 1970, 294–95.
34. Shoup and Hinrichs, 2019.
35. Ibid., 74.
36. Kohlberg, 1976; Kohlberg, 1984.
37. Kidder, 1996.
38. Pojman, 2006, 56.
39. Kohlberg estimated that "less than 20% of American adults reach the principled level of development" (Trevino, 1986, 606). Ishida (2006) reported that "only 20-25% of the adult population ever reaches the last two post-conventional stages" (65). Weber and Green (1991) found that only 23 percent were able to reason at the second stage of level two or above. Rest et al. (2000) reported that higher education levels facilitate the transition to level three.
40. Sternberg, 2019.
41. Bennet, 1995; Adler, 1972.
42. Adler, 1982; Sternberg, *Teaching for Wisdom*, 2015; Maxwell, 2007.
43. Watson, 2019, 304.
44. Engel, 2013.

BIBLIOGRAPHY

Adler, Mortimer. *The Paideia Proposal: An Educational Manifesto.* New York: Simon & Schuster, 1982.

Adler, Mortimer, and Charles Van Doren. *How to Read a Book.* New York: Simon & Schuster, 1972.

Agoramoorthy, Govindasamy. "Spiritual Seekers and Gurus in Contemporary Hindu Society." *Global Society* 51, no. 5 (2014): 558-61.

Akasoy, Anna. "Averroes." In *The Classical Tradition,* edited by Anthony Grafton, Glenn Most, and Salvatore Settis, 111-12. Cambridge, MA: The Belknap Press of Harvard University Press, 2010.

Ali, Abdullah Ysuf. *The Qur'an Translation.* New York: Tahrike Tarsile Qur'an, Inc., 2002.

Anacker, Gayne J., and John Shoup. "Leadership in the Context of the Christian Worldview." In *Organizational Leadership: Foundations and Practices for Christians,* edited by John Burns, John Shoup, and Donald Summons Jr., 35-64. Downers Grove, IL: Intervarsity Press, 2014.

Ansary, Tamim. *Destiny Disrupted: A History of the World through Islamic Eyes.* New York: Public Affairs, 2009.

Ardelt, Monica. "Empirical Assessment of a Three-Dimensional Wisdom Scale." *Research on Aging* 25, no. 3 (2003): 275-324.

Bak, Per. *How Nature Works: The Science of Self-Organized Criticality.* Cambridge, MA: Oxford University Press, 1997.

Baltes, P., and U. Staudinger. "Wisdom: A Metaheuristic (Pragmatic) to Orchestrate Mind and Virtue toward Excellence." *American Psychologist* 55, no. 1 (2000): 122–36.

Baltes, Paul, Judith Glück, and Ute Kunzmann. "Wisdom: Its Structure and Function in Regulating Successful Life Span Development." In *Handbook of Positive Psychology*, edited by C. R. Synder, Shane J. Lopez, Lisa M. Edwards, and Susana C. Marques, 327–47. Cambridge, MA: Oxford University Press, 2002.

Barabási, Albert-László, and Eric Bonabeau. "Scale-free Networks." *Scientific American* 288, no. 5 (2003): 60–69.

Bartholomew, Craig, and Ryan P. O'Dowd. *Old Testament Wisdom Literature: A Theological Introduction.* Westmont, IL: InterVarsity Press Academic, 2011.

Bennett, William. *The Children's Book of Virtues.* New York: Simon & Schuster, 1995.

Black, Deborah. "Alfarabi." In *A Companion to Philosophy in the Middle Ages*, edited by Jorge Gracia and Timothy Noone, 109–117. Malden, MA: Blackwell Publishing Ltd, 2002.

Boethius. *The Consolation of Philosophy.* Translated by Richard H. Green. Reprint, n.p.: Dover Publications Inc., 2002.

Buchanan, Mark. *Ubiquity: The Science of History or Why the World Is Simpler Than We Think.* New York: Three Rivers Press, 2001.

Burrell, David. "Avicenna (Ibn Sīnā)." In *A Companion to Philosophy in the Middle Ages*, edited by Jorge Gracia and Timothy Noone, 196–208. Malden, MA: Blackwell Publishing Ltd., 2002.

Carson, D. A. "Matthew." In *The Expositor's Bible Commentary*, edited by Frank E. Gaebelein. Grand Rapids: Zondervan, 1984.

Chaudhuri, Nirad, Madeleine Biardeau, D. F. Pocock, T. N. Madan. *The Hinduism Omnibus.* Cambridge, MA: Oxford University Press, 2003.

Chung-Ming, Lau, and Richard Woodman. "Understanding Organizational Change: A Schematic Perspective." *Academy of Management Journal* 38, no. 2 (1995): 538.

Clayton, V. P., and J. E. Birren. "The Development of Wisdom Across the Life-Span: A Reexamination of an Ancient Topic." In *Life-Span Development and Behavior*, Vol. 3, edited by Paul B. Baltes and Orville G. Brim Jr., 103–35. Cambridge, MA: Academic Press, 1980.

Connolly, Timothy. "Sagehood and Supererogation in the *Analects*." *Journal of Chinese Philosophy* 40, no. 2 (2013): 269–86.

De Mowbray, Malcolm. "Philosophy as Handmaid of Theology: Biblical Exegesis in the Service of Scholarship." *Traditio* 59 (2004): 1–37.

Dhavamony, Mariasusai. *Classical Hinduism*. Rome: Gregorian & Biblical Press, 1982.

Dweck, Carol. *Mindset: The New Psychology of Success*. New York: Ballantine Books, 2007.

Elayyan, Ribhi Mustafa. "The History of Arabic-Islamic Libraries: 7th to 14th Centuries." *International Library Review* 22, no. 2 (2014): 119–35.

Engel, Susan. "The Case for Curiosity." *Educational Leadership* 70, no. 5 (2013): 36–40.

Epstein, Lee, Jeffrey A. Segal, Harold J. Spaeth, and Thomas G. Walker. *The Supreme Court Compendium: Data, Decisions, and Developments*. 6th ed. Washington, DC: CQ Press, 2015.

Ericsson, K. Anders, Neil Charness, Paul J. Feltovich, and Robert R. Hoffman. 2006. *The Cambridge Handbook of Expertise and Expert Performance*. Cambridge, UK: Cambridge University Press, 2006.

Erikson, Erik H. *Childhood and Society. 35th Anniversary Edition with a New Foreword*. New York: W.W. Norton, 1985.

Erikson, Erik H. *Insight and Responsibility*. New York: W.W. Norton & Company, 1964.

Fakhry, Majid. *A History of Islamic Philosophy*. 3rd ed. New York: Columbia University Press, 2004.

Flood, Gavin. "History of Hinduism." BBC, last modified August 24, 2009, https://www.bbc.co.uk/religion/religions/hinduism/history/history_1.shtml.

Franklin, Benjamin. *The Life and Miscellaneous Writings of Benjamin Franklin*. Edinbrugh: William and Robert Chambers, 1839.

Geisler, Norman, and William D. Watkins. *Worlds Apart: A Handbook on World Views*. 2nd ed. Eugene, OR: Wipf and Stock Publishers, 2003.

Glück, Judith, Susanne König, Katja Naschenweng, Uwe Redzanowski, Lara Dorner, Irene Straßer, and Wolfgang Wiedermann. "How to Measure Wisdom: Content, Reliability, and Validity of Five Measures." *Frontiers in Psychology* 4 (2013): 1–13.

Goodman, Lenn E. *Avicenna*. London: Routledge, 1992.

Gratz v. Bollinger, 539 U.S. 244 (2003).

Grey, Thomas C. "The Constitution as Scripture." *Stanford Law Review* 37, no. 1 (1984): 1–25.

Grutter v. Bollinger, 539 U.S. 306 (2003).

Gutas, Dimitri. "Al-Farabi." In *The Classical Tradition*, edited by Anthony Grafton, Glenn Most, and Salvatore Settis, 20–21. Cambridge, MA: The Belknap Press of Harvard University Press, 2010.

Gutas, Dimitri. "Avicenna." In *The Classical Tradition*, edited by Anthony Grafton, Glenn Most, and Salvatore Settis, 112–14. Cambridge, MA: The Belknap Press of Harvard University Press, 2010.

Hamilton, Alexander. Federalist No. 78, in *The Federalist Papers*. New York: Signet Classics, 2003.

Holliday, Stephen G., and Michael Chandler. *Wisdom: Explorations in Adult Competence*. Contributions to Human Development, 17. Basel and New York: Karger, 1986.

Hume, George Ernest. *The Thirteen Principal Upanishads Translated from the Sanskrit*. London: Forgotten Books, 1931.

Ishida, Chiharu. "How Do Scores of DIT and MJT Differ? A Critical Assessment of the Use of Alternative Moral Development Scales in Studies of Business Ethics." *Journal of Business Ethics* 67 (2006): 63–74.

Jeste, Dilip V., and Ipsit V. Vahia. "Comparison of the Conceptualization of Wisdom in Ancient Indian Literature with Modern Views." *Guildford Press* 71, no. 3 (2008): 197–209.

Joyce, Bruce, Marsha Weil, and Beverly Showers. *Models of Teaching*. 4th ed. New York: Allyn & Bacon, 1992.

Kaufman, James C., and Robert J. Sternberg. *The Cambridge Handbook of Creativity*. Cambridge, UK: Cambridge University Press, 2010.

Keeney, Bradford P. *Aesthetics of Change*. New York: The Guilford Press, 1983.

Keller, Timothy. *The Reason for God: Belief in an Age of Skepticism*. New York: Riverhead Books, 2008.

Khalidi, Tarif. "Introduction," in *The Qur'an*, xii. London: Penguin Books, 2009.

Khrushchev, Nikita S. *Khrushchev Remembers*. Translated by Strobe Talbott. Boston: Little Brown & Company, 1970.

Kidder, Rushworth M. *How Good People Make Tough Choices: Resolving the Dilemmas of Ethical Living*. 1st Fireside ed. New York: Simon & Schuster, 1996.

Koch, Richard. *The 80/20 Principle*. New York: Currency Doubleday, 1998.

Kohlberg, Lawrence. "Moral Stages and Moralization: The Cognitive-Developmental Approach." In *Moral Development and Behavior: Theory, Research and Social Issues*, edited by Thomas Lickona, 31–54. New York: Holt, Rinehart and Winston, 1976.

Kohlberg, Lawrence. *The Psychology of Moral Development: The Nature and Validity of Moral Stages*. Vol. 2 of *Essays on Moral Development*. New York: Harper & Row, 1984.

Kuhn, Thomas S. *The Structure of Scientific Revolutions*. Chicago: University of Chicago Press, 1996.

Leach, Robert. "A Religion of the Book? On Sacred Texts in Hinduism." *Sage Journals* 126, no. 1 (2014): 15–27.

Lennox, John C. *God's Undertaker: Has Science Buried God?* Oxford: Lion, 2009.

Leys, Simon. "Introduction," in *The Analects of Confucius*, xv–xxxii. New York: W.W. Norton & Co. Inc., 1997.

Lincoln, Abraham. "The Gettysburg Address." November 19, 1863, transcript. Abraham Lincoln Online, http://www.abrahamlincolnonline.org/lincoln/speeches/gettysburg.htm.

Madison, James. Federalist No. 10, in *The Federalist Papers*. New York: Signet Classics, 2003.

Madison, James. Federalist No. 51, in *The Federalist Papers*. New York: Signet Classics, 2003.

Martin, John. "Understanding the Confucian *Analects*." *The Library of Congress Information Bulletin* 57, no. 4 (1998).

Maxwell, Nicholas. *From Knowledge to Wisdom: A Revolution for Science and the Humanities*. 2nd ed. London: Pentire Press, 2007.

Mill, John Stuart. *On Liberty*. New Haven: Yale University, 2003.

Mohammed, Ali Haj. "Historical Background of Arab Achievements in the Islamic Golden Age." *Relatórios Técnico/Científicos*, no. 1 (2012).

Moreland, J. P. "How Christian Philosophers Can Serve Systematic Theologians and Biblical Scholars." *Journal of Evangelical Theological Society* 63, no. 2 (2020): 297–306.

Moreland, J. P., and William Lane Craig. *Philosophical Foundations for a Christian Worldview*. Downers Grove, IL: IVP Academic, 2003.

Morgan, Christopher W. *A Theology of James: Wisdom for God's People (Explorations in Biblical Theology)*. Philipsburg, NJ: P& R Publishing, 2010.

Ni, Peimin. *Understanding the Analects of Confucius*. New York: State University of New York Press, 2017.

Ogden, Schubert M. "Theology and Religious Studies: Their Difference and the Difference It Makes." *Journal of the American Academy of Religion* 46, no. 1 (1978): 3–17.

Ohno, Taiichi. *Toyota Production System: Beyond Large Scale Production*. Boca Raton: CRC Press, 1988.

Osborne, Grant R. *The Hermeneutical Spiral: A Comprehensive Introduction to Biblical Interpretation*. Downers Grove, IL: Intervarsity Press, 1997.

Owens, Mackubin Thomas. "The Wisdom of the Constitution and the Declaration of Independence." *The Institute of World Politics*. Last modified September 17, 2015. https://www.iwp.edu/speeches-lectures/2015/09/17/the-wisdom-of-the-constitution-and-the-declaration-of-independence/.

Pasnau, Robert. "The Islamic Scholar Who Gave Us Modern Philosophy." *Humanities* 32, no. 6 (2011): 34–51.

Paulsen, Michael S., and Luke Paulsen. *The Constitution: An Introduction.* New York: Basic Books, 2015.

Peterson, Christopher, and Martin E. P. Seligman. *Character Strengths and Virtues: A Handbook and Classification.* Oxford, UK: American Psychological Association and Oxford University Press, 2004.

Pojman, Louis P. *Ethics: Discovering Right and Wrong.* 5th ed. Belmont, CA: Thomson Wadsworth, 2006.

Poplin, Mary. *Is Reality Secular: Testing the Assumptions of Four Global Worldviews.* Downers Grove, IL: IVP Books, 2014.

Reck, Andrew J. "The Philosophical Background of the American Constitution." *Royal Institute of Philosophy Supplement* 19 (1985): 273–93.

Reiss, Edmund. *Boethius.* Woodbridge, CT: Twayne Publishers, 1982.

Renima, Ahmed, Habib Tiliouine, and Richard J. Estes. "The Islamic Golden Age: A Story of Triumph of the Islamic Civilization." In *The State of Social Progress of Islamic Societies*, edited by Habib Tiliouine and Richard Estes, 25–52. Berlin: Springer, 2016.

Rest, James R., Darcia Narvaez, Stephen J. Thoma, and Muriel J. Bebeau. "A Neo-Kohlbergian Approach to Morality Research." *Journal of Moral Education* 29, no. 4 (2000): 381–95.

Rubenstein, Richard E. *Aristotle's Children: How Christians, Muslims, and Jews Rediscovered Ancient Wisdom and Illuminated the Middle Ages.* Orlando, FL: Harcourt, Inc., 2003.

Russell, Bertrand. *History of Western Philosophy.* Milton, UK: Taylor & Francis, 2004.

Russell, Bertrand. *The Problems of Philosophy.* Oxford, UK: Oxford University, 2001.

Saxe, John Godfrey. *The Blind Men and the Elephant.* CommonLit. Accessed January 11, 2021, https://www.commonlit.org/texts/the-blind-men-and-the-elephant.

Schwartz, Barry, and Kenneth Sharpe. *Practical Wisdom: The Right Way to Do the Right Thing.* New York: Riverhead Books, 2010.

Shendruk, Amanda. "Fewer than 2% of Supreme Court Rulings Are Ever Overturned." Quartz Media, Inc. Last modified July 14, 2018. https://qz.com/1326096/despite-its-pending-hard-right-turn-the-supreme-court-is-unlikely-to-overturn-roe-vs-wade/.

Shoup, John R., and Troy W. Hinrichs. *Literature and Leadership: The Role of the Narrative in Organizational Sensemaking.* London: Routledge, 2019.

Shoup, John R., and Susan Clark Studer. *Leveraging Chaos: The Mysteries of Leadership and Policy Revealed.* Lanham, MD: Rowman & Littlefield Education, 2010.

Slingerland, Edward. *Confucius Analects: With Selection from Traditional Commentaries.* Indianapolis: Hackett Publishing Company, 2003.

Smith, Brian K. "Canonical Authority and Social Classification: Veda and 'Varna' in Ancient Indian Texts." *History of Religions 32*, no. 2 (1992): 103–25.

Staudinger, Ursula M. "The Need to Distinguish Personal from General Wisdom: A Short History of Empirical Evidence." In *The Scientific Study of Personal Wisdom: From Contemplative Traditions to Neuroscience*, edited by Michel Ferrari and Nic M. Weststrate, 3–20. Berlin: Springer, 2013.

Sternberg, Robert J. "Personal Wisdom in the Balance." In *The Scientific Study of Personal Wisdom: From Contemplative Traditions to Neuroscience*, edited by Michel Ferrari and Nic M. Weststrate, 53–74. Berlin: Springer, 2013.

Sternberg, Robert J. "Still Searching for the Zipperump-a-Zoo: A Reflection After 40 Years." *Child Development Perspectives 9*, no. 2 (2015): 106–10.

Sternberg, Robert J. *Teaching for Wisdom, Intelligence, Creativity, and Success.* New York: Skyhorse Publishing, 2015.

Sternberg, Robert J. "What Is Wisdom and How Can We Develop It?" *The Annals of the American Academy of Political and Social Science 591*, no. 1 (2004): 164–74.

Sternberg, Robert J. "Why People Often Prefer Wise Guys to Guys Who Are Wise: An Augmented Balance Theory of the Production and Reception of Wisdom." In *The Cambridge Handbook of Wisdom*, edited by Robert J. Sternberg and Judith Glück, 162–81. Cambridge, MA: Cambridge University Press, 2019.

Sternberg, Robert J. "Wisdom and Its Relations to Intelligence and Creativity." In *Wisdom: Its Nature, Origins, and Development*, edited by Robert J. Sternberg, 142–59. Cambridge, MA: Cambridge University Press, 1990.

Sternberg, Robert J. *Wisdom, Intelligence, and Creativity Synthesized.* Cambridge, MA: Cambridge University Press, 2003.

Sternberg, Robert J., & The Rainbow Project Collaborators. "The Rainbow Project: Enhancing the SAT through Assessments of Analytical, Practical, and Creative Skills." *Intelligence 34* (2006): 321–50.

Stokes, Donald E., and Gudmund R. Iversen. "On the Existence of Forces Restoring Party Competition." *Public Opinion Quarterly 26*, no. 2 (1962): 159–71.

Supreme Court Procedures, United States Courts. Accessed April 14, 2021, https://www.uscourts.gov/about-federal-courts/educational-resources/about-educational-outreach/activity-resources/supreme-1.

Taylor, A. E. *Plato: The Man and His Work.* Berlin: Routledge, 2012.

Taylor, Richard C. "Averroes." In *A Companion to Philosophy in the Middle Ages*, edited by Jorge J. E. Gracia and Timothy B. Noone, 182–95. Hoboken, NJ: Blackwell Publishing Ltd., 2002.

Trevino, Linda Klebe. "Ethical Decision Making in Organizations: A Person-Situation Interactionist Model." *The Academy of Management Review* 11, no. 3 (1986): 601–17.

Watson, Lani. "Educating for Inquisitiveness: A Case Against Exemplarism for Intellectual Character Education." *Journal of Moral Education* 48, no. 3 (2019): 303–15.

Watzlawick, Paul, John H. Weakland, and Richard Fisch. *Change; Principles of Problem Formation and Problem Resolution.* New York: W.W. Norton & Company, Inc., 1974.

Weber, James, and Sharon Green. "Principled Moral Reasoning: Is It a Viable Approach to Promote Ethical Integrity?" *Journal of Business Ethics* 10, no. 5 (1991): 325–33.

Werther, David, and Susan Werther, ed. *C.S. Lewis's List: The Ten Books That Influenced Him Most.* New York: Bloomsbury Academic, 2015.

Willmington, Harold L. "What You Need to Know about the Book of Proverbs." Liberty University. Published in 2009. http://digitalcommons.liberty.edu/will_know/51.

Worthing, Mark William. "Theology: Queen of the Sciences?" *Concordia Journal* 20 no. 4 (1994): 402–14.

Young, William A. *The World's Religions: Worldviews and Contemporary Issues,* 3rd ed. Hoboken, NJ: Prentice Hall, 2010.

Yu, Jiyuan. "*Yi*: Practical Wisdom in Confucius's Analects." *Journal of Chinese Philosophy* 33 (2006): 335–48.

Zingher, Joshua N. "The Ideological and Electoral Determinants of Laws Targeting Undocumented Migrants in the U.S." *State Politics & Policy Quarterly* 14, no. 1 (2014): 90–117.

INDEX

INDEX

individual soul (*atman* or soul), 52
Individual *versus* Community, right-
versus-right dilemma, 108
Industrial Revolution, 59
injustice, Boethius on, 4
intellect (*nous*), 12
intellectual virtues, 12, 93
intelligence, 68, 69, 70, 75
intelligent people, 62–63, 68
interpersonal dynamics, and wisdom,
70–71
invariable truth, variable truth
contrasted with, 12
invisible and visible truths, wisdom
balances, 93
IQ, global conflict and, 69
Ishida, Chiharu, 127n37
Islam (submission)
five pillars of, 45, 122n20
Golden Age of, 21
Hinduism contrasted with, 49
libraries of, 22
philosophers of, 21–25
Islamic *falasifa* (philosophy), Hellenic
philosophy and, 23
Israel, 34, 35, 36, 121n11

Jesus, 121n4
crucifixion and resurrection of, 41
on Kingdom of God, 41, 42, 44
the Quran recognizing, 45
Sermon on the Mount of, 33–34, 43
in the wilderness, 43
Judaism, Hinduism contrasted with, 49
See also Hebrew Bible
Judge, all-seeing and Benevolent, 5
judgment
understanding through contemplative,
8, 19

wisdom and, 82
junzi (gentleman), 18
justice, individual and societal, 6–8, 11,
74, 75
justifying God (*theodicy*), 37

karma (previous deeds of individuals),
53, 54, 55
Kaufman, James C., 70
Ketuvi'im. *See* writings
Khalid, Tarif, 48
Khrushchev, Nikita, 102–3
Kidder, Rushworth, 108
Kingdom of God, 41, 42, 44
knowing, 59, 70, 71, 90, 92
of God, 51, 52
God as all-, 5, 38–39
not knowing and, 89
theology ultimate source of, 25
thinking *versus*, 65
knowledge, as precursor to
understanding, 84
Koch, Richard, 77
Kohlberg, Lawrence, 107–8, 109,
127n37
Kongzi (The Master) or Kong Zi
(Master Kong). *See* Confucius
Krishna (lord), 54–55, 123n47

Lady Philosophy, of Boethius, 3, 4, 5,
121n7
law of the harvest, in wisdom
literature, 32
laws, virtue promoted through, 9
The Laws (Plato), 9, 118n25
leaders and leadership, vii, ix, 19–20
learning, in the *Analects*, 16
l'esprit de l'escalier (spirit of the
staircase), 107